Dedication

This book is dedicated to all the teachers in my life: those encountered during my formal education, those I work with, and those who I learn from just through living and loving.

Lynnbeth Ford
October 2020

Table of Contents

Acknowledgments and a Word from the Author

This isn't your typical section of acknowledgments because I want to talk a bit about the situation regarding the times in which we currently live. I'll speak more about this in the introduction, too.

The COVID-19 quarantine is (at the time of this writing, in early May 2020) in its 7th week in Vancouver, B.C., Canada, which is where I live. We shut down fairly early and as a result, we have a reasonably low incidence of death here in western Canada. The United States has just passed the 56,000-death mark, with no end in sight (as of May 10, 2020, there were 78,771 deaths). Several southern states plan on opening their economies soon (some already have). It is a scary time we are living in. We are now more aware of details about this particular strain of the Coronavirus. We know that people are carriers before they are symptomatic, we do not have enough testing to know who has the disease, the early rumors of young people not getting it are false, and more. Fear is growing. Fear and anxiety of not knowing, not having control, and being a possible victim are causing people to have confusing emotions.

How everything changed so fast—overnight, really—is astounding. The first reaction I had was similar to everyone else—something like "the sky is falling… oops, there it is on the floor!" After processing some of what has become "the new 'normal,'" I feel much more organized, I appreciate my health and wellness so much, and I feel like I am making stronger connections with all the people in my life.

The situation has given many of us a forced look at possibilities that we may never have experienced otherwise. These include things like suspending or stopping air travel, having no cars on the road, people being forced to spend time with their families, and isolating or quarantining ourselves.

However, Earth is getting a huge breather and air pollution all over the world is clearing up. Globally, this is a good thing. As you will see in the coming pages, the human ecology of health and wellness—where everything is clearly connected like a giant mobile—has also found some space, however little, amidst the pandemic. This is good news because it is possible that the dire climate predictions need not come true. We have choices, knowledge, and an opportunity to see various possibilities for our future, especially when we all buy into a profound idea and work together to make wonderful things happen!

I also want to acknowledge how and why this book came into existence. After my lengthy recovery from near fatal appendicitis and sepsis, this book began in earnest, in 2017, after watching David Suzuki's *The Nature of Things—It Takes Guts*, on CBC TV. This television episode brought together many scientists and their microbiome research into my living room. It spoke to me in a way that I embraced. I had no idea then how much of an impact this information would make on my life.

First, I began to understand my own complex medical history. Second, I began to uncover and then connect all the information herein, initially to my own health and life, and then to the symptoms of those around me. This new learning was added on top of my foundational "Land, Food and Community" education from University of British Columbia, my Human Ecology education, and my personal journey to regain health. The microbiome learning grew organically through my own experience and research, to where I now teach and speak about it to educate and help others. Through my *It Takes Guts* experience, I learned I need to concentrate on feeding my personal microbiome, so I "cracked the code" to my own recovery and health. I am forever grateful, Dr. Suzuki!

I am also indebted to my doctor, Dr. Heli McPhie, who continues to guide me on my personal healing journey. She said to me, smiling matter-of-factly, one day, "Lynne, you really should write a book." Here it finally is. I look forward to writing the next one together.

Preface

May 1, 2020. As I set down to polish off this final draft before it is sent to my editor, my partner and I are enjoying our 7th week of isolation. We get to live and work at home, in a very small apartment, with our dog and cat, watching the Cuomo brothers on CNN every day—and Trudeau, and of course, Trump. Some days, we are hooked on the news morning, noon, and night, because it is so gripping, frightening, and incredibly life-changing. What a rapidly-changing world we are living in right now!

Every day, at the beginning of this pandemic, there was some crisis!

I know that this period of time will go down in history. Bill Gates was doing an interview last night and he mentioned something about how we are already getting used to the "new normal" and we will forever look back at this time as a major event. He gave the example of watching a movie on TV where people were shaking hands and how abnormal that appeared already. We know it was not made this year! We are already creating the new normal by observing the contrast.

I hope, looking back on this time, that we can see where we did our best, how we coped with life in spite of adversity, and that we made the world a better place because of the stark contrast we are experiencing. Some people say we will never go back to the way it was. The new normal has no handshakes or hugs, and no kissing first one cheek, then the other, and then back again, like they did in France. Masks are a part of our lives, now.

By watching the news and hearing the statistics as well as perusing the new research that is currently emerging, we can see that there is even more evidence of how important the ideas are outlined around the gut microbiome and the connection to our brain. The "second brain" concept and the power of the healthy gut-brain-microbiome connection is literally cutting edge. We shall soon see where this new research takes us.

I sense a stronger connection between the gut, brain, and immunity than we even realized a few short weeks ago. Every day, as more data is gathered, it becomes more apparent that those most greatly affected by COVID-19 are the elderly and those who have pre-existing conditions that have lifestyle implications, such as Diabetes, heart disease, and lung issues. Although these are terrible diseases, many are exacerbated by poor food choices and other bad habits such as too much drinking, smoking, and overeating.

There are studies being done on those who have passed away and there is preliminary autopsy information. There are questions, too. Why do some people have different symptoms than others? Why are some carriers asymptomatic? What are the indicators of immunity for those who don't get sick but have the virus? Why are some people immune? How do we build an immunity for the prevention of such a disease?

A bigger question is: how can we, as a society, work more on the building of our health rather than on the economics of industrial processed and factory-farmed food that is grown and made for production and consumer convenience?

I hope we all discover and realize the answers to these questions, because a new world can and may emerge from this pandemic, where drugs may no longer be as necessary—a world where we can and do harness our gift of natural wellness and learn to use the human gut microbiome for its full potential and purpose.

I foresee us keeping our health through proper food, building our immunities, improving our mental health, and controlling the obesity epidemic that is also rampant in this time.

Introduction

This book is the result of a substantial research that is combined with a journey of discovery that began with my naturopathic doctor before the year 2000. I have suffered from arthritis for many years. As I look back over my life, I am sure I had chronic inflammation first, and I truly suspect it has been part of my life since adolescence.

Since my first major knee injury in 1982 to my toe surgery in 2016, I have had so many operations and doses of antibiotics that I lost count. Some surgeries were for urgent injuries, some were for arthritic damaged joints, and some were for other issues. I can now see, in hindsight, after all the reading and research I have done, all of the various symptoms that have caused me health issues come from inflammation. Inflammation has actually become the call sign for most diseases, in modern times.

It seems counterintuitive that a skin disease such as eczema or psoriasis can have the same source as something like anxiety, arthritis, weight gain, or constantly getting colds, but this is exactly what research is now telling us.

Through my personal story, and using the Human Ecological Model as a guide, the material in this book is organized so we can begin to understand the multitude of influences and pressures on human health and wellness. Here, we follow the various internal and external environments that pressure not only our personal health, but the health of all organisms on the planet. Everything is related and interconnected.

Going through how our near and our distant environmental relationships are interconnected can give us a new perspective on how we CAN effect change in the world. That change can happen by first taking care of our own body and our own space, then it will naturally progress from there.

Through the lens of the Human Ecological Model, we can see how "the butterfly effect" of the small independent acts of simple things such as daily food choices can completely change the way of the world for ourselves and literally billions of others.

This book is about feeding and caring for your microbiome. It is organized as a comprehensive resource to save you time and energy as you learn and maybe share the science of this information. By gathering this vast amount of research into one small handbook, this book is small but powerful. Videos, discussions, and recipes are readily available to support learning and practice. This book is about feeding and caring for your microbiome. It is organized as a comprehensive resource to save you time and energy as you learn and maybe share the science of this information.

The bottom line is that we can change our planet as individuals from the bottom up, by learning about our own health and wellness.

Our daily habits affect everything and everyone around us. You may already have an idea of what the microbiome really means, but probably no specifics. It is possible you have enough information to recognize that you need a "handbook," which may come from a specific reason for reading this type of book right now. Maybe your child has some difficulty with concentration or digestion—or both. Perhaps you are a teacher with an interest in the health of your students and colleagues, and this book seemed to have some answers. Are you looking for inspiration or guidance on how to change the eating habits of your school's children, your own children, or your family members? Have you heard snippets about something called the microbiome and wonder if this could help? After all, there are commercials on television with products—everything from flavoured water to skin cream—that mention the benefits of the microbiome. What is it, what is the big deal, and why is it everywhere, all of a sudden?

If any of these ideas ring true or sound familiar, keep reading. There are a lot of reasons you may have picked this book up. These reasons have a connection because there are many different "on ramps" to this common denominator, as you will soon see. If you take a look at the questions posed here, you may see more interrelationships that you had not considered before.

For example, does someone you know have a serious skin condition such as psoriasis or eczema? Maybe another person experiences a stomach ailment. Do you have nausea, heartburn, indigestion, upset stomach, or diarrhea? That sounds like a commercial, but there are thousands of people who take remedies for symptoms like these every day. And although temporary relief may result, the real or underlying problems are not solved. Evidence of this kind of thinking is obvious when watching the never-ending lists of side-effects when watching Big Pharma commercials on TV.

Perhaps someone you know has a recently escalated anxiety problem that originally seemed trivial. Suddenly, they suffered a panic attack and one grew into many. Now, the fear of another attack has curbed their behavior or caused an avoidance of certain situations.

Does someone you know have a long-term history of taking medications? If they have tried to reduce or quit taking them, did they have severe reactions?

Perhaps you know a person who, without warning, developed an allergy or a rash, or gained weight rapidly and without explanation after being ill. Sometimes, an allergy will go wild, resulting in multiple allergies, the body covered in hives, and hospitalization. This can be very scary and sometimes leaves individuals afraid of eating anything for fear of another severe reaction.

Say a relative develops a serious autoimmune disease such as celiac, Hashimoto's, or arthritis. Perhaps another family member is in the beginning stages of Multiple Sclerosis (MS) or Alzheimer's. These diseases are on the rapid increase and many of us are wondering why all of this is happening. Why is it that so many people are getting serious diseases of this sort now? Is it because we are getting better at diagnosing them? This is partially true, but there are dramatic increases in all sorts of diseases that have been rare in the past.

If anyone you care about has issues with immunity, obesity, or mood/mental health, consider that you can help support their overall healing process by increasing their consumption of good, whole, healthy foods—particularly, fermented foods. Does it shock you that food is the answer? Really, how could it be that simple? Remember the phrase "garbage in, garbage out"?

All of this may appear mainstream to you, if you have been exploring new scientific information. If it sounds far-fetched that all of these maladies are completely unrelated, they—surprisingly—are not. Specifically, as you will find by reading this book, changing food-related habits in small ways can have major effects on your entire family's health, through direct feeding and care of your household's collective gut microbiome.

You may witness a variety of illness or symptoms in family and friends around you. Interestingly, in different generations, symptoms may appear completely different, but they, in fact, may have a connecting factor in the gut. Presentations of all of these afflictions are as different "diseases" but they actually ARE NOT completely different diseases. There is a huge chance that these symptoms ARE related through a recently discovered "organ" in our bodies—our human gut microbiome.

The Food-Mood Connection: A Holistic Approach to Understanding the Gut-Brain-Microbiome Relationship demonstrates that all of these diseases can appear to be unrelated because they present as symptoms in completely different parts of the human body. These symptoms are an expression of an inflammation that has travelled through the bloodstream to a particularly vulnerable area. For example, a rash is a skin issue—or so we thought. We normally ask our general practitioner to send us to a specialist, such as a dermatologist, for a skin problem. The skin doctor will usually treat the problem with a cream that likely contains a steroid, never actually solving the issue with the gut.

Now, imagine the following scenarios.

Your child is hyperactive or just distracted at home, but behaviors are consistently enough of a concern at school that the teacher brings it to your and other teachers' attention. Behavioral issues are too much to handle in the classroom. Therefore, outside professional consultation is recommended.

You comply with the direction, as you understand there is a problem, but are unsure how to handle it at home. Often individual or family counselling can help considerably. However, symptoms may grow, unexplained. What are you to do?

Another child, a "picky eater" recently diagnosed with Autism, has known digestive and elimination issues. Restrictive eating is likely one of the solutions. "Craves carbs" is the most common anecdotal evidence of the problem.

Did you know that over 90% of autistic patients have gut issues? How is that important? With the scary predictions of the growth of statistics of children with Autism in the near future, this is a major concern for the families of these children, the support necessary in schools, and for the healthcare system.

If you are part of the "Sandwich Generation" (who cares for aging parents while taking care of your own children and dealing with their issues), your hands are full. You were not totally aware of how your parents were eating or taking care of themselves. When one of them showed signs of physical or cognitive decline, you realized they were living on tea, toast, and TV dinners. Who knew that their health issues were actually related to their gut issues?

Recent science has discovered the decline of the human gut microbiome is the underlying thread in the rise of many diseases. Yet, we didn't even know much about the *gut microbiome* and its importance in our health until recently—in the past 10 years.

In light of the challenging times we now live in, the importance of taking responsibility for our own health is paramount. Not only must we understand what health is and how to create it in ourselves, we must clearly know how to practically aid our own bodies in our own immunity and mental health. We also must take control of obesity in our society. We now know for sure that these issues are all related to food and are largely preventable.

The past few months of social distancing, quarantine, and self-isolation have shown how fragile our mental health can be. Anecdotally, the news carries stories from one extreme to the other. For example, the largest baby boom since the 1950s is predicted to happen in 2021, as are spikes in the amount of domestic abuse, separations, and divorce. Alcohol and recreational drug use has increased dramatically, as have prescription drug use and opioid overdoses. We are already chronically mentally strained and this pandemic has put many people in serious trouble with their mental health.

People are smoking, drinking, eating, and sitting more because the gyms, beaches, parks, playgrounds, and hiking trails are closed. Conducting socialization as well as business via Zoom meetings or conferences has been an overnight sensation. All of this adds up to not eating right, not exercising properly, and stressing about how to pay the bills (and find a new job, in many cases).

This book will teach you what you need to know about the gut-brain-microbiome relationship and how it can reboot your mental health, improve your immune system, and help you overcome obesity. (Note that the references for the numbers that appear in superscript in this book are numerically listed in order in the REFERENCES section.)

Chapter 1: What is the Human Gut Microbiome?

The microbiome is a collection of trillions of bacteria, viruses, protozoa, fungi, and other microscopic life who live together in our intestinal tract. Some are "resident," meaning that they establish themselves and hang out for long periods of time, and some are "transient" or come for a good time, not a long time. This community ebbs and flows. It grows and changes, depending on the types of foods we eat and the "bugs" we consume, either accidentally or on purpose. The microbiome has probably remained fairly consistent over millennia, although varying and changing with nomadic versus agricultural lifestyles as well as local and seasonal food availability. We are now quite sure that our microbiome has been under assault and is suffering.

Since the Second World War, we have experienced a huge rise in the use of antibiotics and chemicals for food crops in fertilizers and pest control all over the world. We have— alongside the food system issues—witnessed our society become extremely "germ-phobic." We battle "bad bacteria" all around us, from antibiotics (to combat disease) to antiseptic cleaners (to combat household germs). Mr. Clean is a well-known commercial character. We have been conditioned to fear germs and bad bacteria all around us. We are not taught about "good bacteria." It is time to change that. We need them desperately.

The importance of gut health to our overall human health was originally discovered by Ilya Ilyich Mechnikov[1] (1845-1916). Mechnikov coined the term "dysbiosis" (also called dysbacteriosis), which is a description of unbalanced gut bacteria—too many bad ones and not enough good ones. He conducted a large amount of research while working at the Pasteur Institute in France near the turn of the 20th century. After his wife died of typhoid, he, at a high risk, experimented by self-inoculating with typhoid and other pathogens. He survived all of them. In an iconic turn of events, penicillin was developed, and his immunological research was tossed out with the bath water... until recently.

The Human Gut Microbiome is the "darling" of current science. Thousands of papers are being published annually from a myriad of medical health journals in many different specialties—all seemingly unrelated to each other. As each medical specialty looks deeper into the microbiome connection to their particular part of anatomy, connections to microbes and the microbiome are being made that were not even seen before. It is now generally accepted that this "new organ" (the microbiome)—the gut microbiome, in particular—is involved in every system and organ of our bodies.

Some call the microbiome our "second brain," which is the basis of the foundation of this science and book. The gut-brain connection accepts that our gut and brain were connected in the beginning of fetal development.

As we develop in utero, the gut and brain grow apart but stay connected through the nervous system. The gut and brain communicate both ways, constantly. It used to be thought the brain communicated to the gut, but it has been proven that the gut talks to the brain as well and our gut has a huge effect on our thoughts, our feelings, and our behaviors.

When studying nutrition and health sciences in university, as students, we learned nothing about *probiotics or prebiotics*. We learned fiber was good for us, translating into eating lots of fruits and vegetables. That's a reasonable takeaway. We were taught of fiber in terms of providing bulk for creating easily excreted waste, for example. We didn't learn anything about *antibiotics* either. Although antibiotics were prescribed throughout my generation for nearly every affliction, including colds, influenza, and viruses, we didn't know it was a bad thing. For example, I was given a very long course of tetracycline for acne when I was 15 and 16 years old. This habit among the entire medical profession in North America has led to a complete over-prescription of these drugs, both for humans and domestic animals, which has resulted in a fairly quick rise in antibiotic resistance, superbugs, and the fear that we will not be able to defeat those strong bad bugs in the future.

When I reflect back, the antibiotic use I was subjected to probably began a long cascade of hormonal and obesity issues throughout my lifetime. Around adolescence, I began to gain weight and experience abnormalities in my cycles, which persisted throughout my entire life.

During my university undergraduate degree, the underlying theme of our nutritional education promoted a low-fat diet. This was quite normal and widely accepted at the time, and in fact many people still believe this. Much emphasis was given to the fact that all fats have twice as much caloric value (by weight) than protein or carbohydrates, for the same amount of food.

As a result, most of my adult life was spent avoiding and being afraid of eating fats. I avoided eating nuts and butter for years because of the nutrient (fat) density and fear of gaining weight. Despite being a member of Weight Watchers from the time I was about 16 years old, I continued to gain weight slowly but surely. University students learn how vitamins and minerals are essential for well-being, but we were not taught anything about how we need our symbiotic microbial friends to help us digest and extract these nutrients in our digestion.

Fiber—namely fruits, vegetables, oats, and other whole grains—was highly promoted in university. We were taught oats and other whole grains were good for moving food through the digestive tract quickly and smoothly. Oats gained popularity and became known for removing cholesterol.

Fiber keeps us full and somehow eating more fiber made it easier to lose weight. The fact is that fiber has become an actual cornerstone for human health, with and from the assistance of the good bacteria in our gastrointestinal system. Without our gut's microbiome and the bacterial by-products, our immunity, our nutrition, weight and even our mental health decline or suffer.

Our immunity—from the common cold to cancer—has connections to the microbiome. Latest studies have shown the microbiome composition changes before many disease onsets, including heart disease, stroke, and cancer. Daily, more and more papers are published in a variety of medical and science journals on the benefits of a healthy and diverse bacteria in our gut. In order to prevent and cure a myriad of human disease, it is becoming clearer that a healthy and diverse microbiome is essential.

Weight management under control used to mean that calories in versus calories out are in balance. This may no longer be true, as our microbiome affects how much food we burn and how much we store.

The microbiome has a huge effect on our mitochondria and metabolism. Additionally, it seems that these certain good bugs and bad bugs are present during certain times and weight trends, but they may even cause as well as affect certain fluctuations.

Food and mood have a strong connection to the microbiome[2]. From ADD, ADHD, anxiety, and depression through to Multiple Sclerosis, Parkinson's, and Alzheimer's, food affects our brain's health—not just through the nutritional value of the food, as has been believed, but through the chemistry of the microbes in our gut! This has been proven through countless studies and now, we must change how we look at and treat mental health in the future.

Lately, studies have shown that certain microbes appear to be responsible for particular biological functions. There are actually databases available now, to indicate which probiotic supplements can affect what affliction. This has become the focal point of much of the current research, yet the correlation appears to be very complex. The correlation appears to depend on the individual because not every application precipitates the same results across the board.

Depending on the foundation of biome you initially possess, results can fluctuate as to the response you receive from a particular strain. There are combinations of microbes that work well together and others that don't. Further studies are required in this area, but the research is promising. It looks like this information is on the cusp of revolutionizing the medical system as we know it.

However, it is now understood our gut bugs are absolutely essential components of *almost every chemical equation happening in our body's systems at the cellular level*. We need them and they need us. In our western society, where we can get what we want when we want it, we need to pay more attention to feeding our microbiome instead of feeding ourselves what we like or don't like. This change is actually essential for our health, our microbes' health, and throughout the chain of life on the planet.

We are in "symbiosis" with this microbiome in our gut. "Symbiosis" means that we are co-dependent and actually *need each other* to survive.

We have not yet fully awakened to how our food, chemicals in farming and pest control, cleaning supplies, and beauty products have contributed to the microbiome's steady demise over the last 100 years. This decline and reduction of diversity in our microbiome is contributing to the rise in many human diseases.

The Food-Mood Connection: A Holistic Approach to Understanding the Gut-Brain-Microbiome Relationship explains the absolute importance of caring for and feeding our own unique microbiome. Each person and family's collective microbiome are slightly different, so there is no "one size fits all" solution. The microbiome's health—and consequently, our health—ultimately depends on how we feed and nurture it. Knowing how to feed this "organ"—a conglomerate of trillions of bacteria, yeasts, fungi, viruses, and protozoa—is essential to our symbiotic health. We need them as much as they need us.

We have been on a road of eradication in the last 50-70 years, without knowing or understanding what we are doing. Its importance has been forgotten—until recently.

This book explains what probiotics, prebiotics, and antibiotics are, and the functionality each group plays in our overall health. The dramatic connection of our gut-brain-axis is also discussed, so as to understand how to deal with symptoms which can appear unrelated but are not. The problems we face as a modern society are all interconnected.

It looks more and more like that the microbiomes of various environments on Earth are at the crux of breakdown. We can only be on the brink for so long. We must take a bottom-up approach to solving our environmental problems, both inside and outside of ourselves. Like a foundation of a house, if each individual functions at a certain level, this process will build on itself, throughout society. Given guidelines at the bottom as well as from the top, we can create anew.

For too long, we, as a culture, have taken our personal health for granted and trusted our social systems as healthy and right. For generations now, our children have had less disease and more life expectancy than the generation before. This is because we have discovered causes of disease and infection.

Progressions in sanitation and farming practices have lessened disease outbreaks, improved crop yields, and given our species the possibilities of fuller and longer lives—until now. In the last 10-20 years, this trend is no longer true. Our children are no longer expected to live a longer lifespan than their parents. Life expectancy is now reducing in the developed world, due to environmental damage and the lack of nutrients in soil and water.

We have believed in our doctors and medical system, and have turned to pharmaceuticals and surgeries as our backstop in solving health issues. We trust our food systems, our governments, and businesses to decide policies for us. We have trusted those in positions of power to know what they are doing in setting laws and processes, so that we are inherently taken care of. Unfortunately, we cannot continue this way any longer.

Everything in the food system, especially in North America, is based on economic decisions and not necessarily on health and wellness, despite consumers thinking this is so. Farming practices and yields are designed to support consistent farmer income. Crops are sprayed with chemicals that kill pests, to increase yields, but as a "carpet bomb," they also destroy the very microbes that promote health of plants and soil. Genetically Modified Organism (GMO) development is rushed through research stages, so care is not taken for long-term evaluation as it is in Europe, where GMOs are prohibited.

Food companies have taken steps since the development of processed foods, to create products based solely on taste and profit—*not health*. Food products and processing are not regulated to make health decisions a higher priority over taste, visual appeal, and shelf-life. If the former were true, then fructose corn syrup would be regulated to be added to any product, for example. Food processing has taken natural nutrients out of foods and replaced them largely with sugars—or worse, artificial sweeteners. Often, these contain chemical additives, to compensate for removing fats. Fats were reduced in foods since the 1980s Canada's Food Guide, because not only do they have more calories per gram, but fats go rancid quickly, so adding them reduces the shelf-life of processed foods. These additives cause issues in our bodies, at the cellular level. Thus, it can take a long time to identify the root cause of arising issues and the link to rising rates of disease. In industry, economic influence takes precedence over decisions based on health. We, as consumers, must make better choices.

Consumers are not generally well-educated about food, even simply how to plant a vegetable garden, shop for good food, cook basic fare, and eat for health. One of the causes is that over the past 50 years, we have largely eliminated basic education in elementary and high schools about food and consumerism in North America. At the university level, courses in Home Economics have closed over and over again across the country, identified as not being important enough or deemed more suited to college level education versus university. There have been fewer and fewer school boards (with parental pressure) in North America who value education in food and cooking over science and math in grade school education.

Education has focused on science and math, to prepare someone for the job market. Learning about health, home, and family life is assumed to be a home-based family education, which has seen a great decline due to the increasing cost of living and pressures on women to work outside the home. Even though it is essential for the equality of women to receive a post-secondary education and have viable professions outside the home, what has historically been practical skills and knowledge coming from home has severely dwindled. This includes practical experience in consumer knowledge, financial literacy, food systems, and human growth and development. The importance of these things as what could in the past be considered a parent's responsibility seems to be not highly valued or reflected in many school boards' funding in North America. For example, the placing of great importance on math and science and the undervaluing of food and physical education and exercise has contributed to widespread obesity and Diabetes. The greatest loss in this is how the lack of these basic human competency skills and knowledge affects the long-term health of our modern society.

The past 10 years have shown a turnaround and increase in programs for junior chefs and gardening in schools, which parallels the surge in cooking shows on television. However, despite these pockets of hope and individual championship, in some states and provinces, nutrition and day-to-day life skills have continually dropped to the bottom of the totem pole in their valuableness of higher education. It's important to acknowledge there are some Home Economics education "holdout areas" where this subject matter is still consistently taught in American states and in my home country, Canada. This has been due largely to dedicated teachers and professionals who continually stand guard on protecting and even expanding the curriculum and budget for support of education of this kind.

Currently, after a few generations of less school funding and more of a focus on job preparation than life preparation, many families don't cook their own food more than once or twice a week. This trend has been steadily increasing to the point where a slim few families have access to backyard gardens, when they were common just 50 years ago.

Nowadays, very few families eat together at home regularly, even just one meal per day. Overscheduled children eat on the run after school, *en route* to piano or soccer, and "carpool" is a verb because most children no longer walk to school. Services such as SkipTheDishes, a takeout delivery service, will now go to any restaurant in town, pick up take-out orders for you, and deliver them straight to your home. Even McDonald's will deliver to homes now! During the current pandemic, almost every restaurant began a takeout service overnight—just to survive. The general population was actively encouraged to buy from all restaurants, to ensure our local favorites survived the COVID-19 outbreak. The bottom line is that we don't even have to go outside to a restaurant or a drive-thru to eat fast food!

This book not only explains how we got to this point in our food systems, but how it is now up to all of us—at the family level—to begin to change it. The family unit is the basic module unit of our society. Our economy is fueled by the decisions that family members or consumers make on a daily basis.

Oprah said years ago, "Once we know better, we do better," and frankly, we must.

When normal everyday people understand how everything is interconnected, we will all move slowly towards a *preventative and healing* health care system. The system starts at the grass roots level, with all of us taking responsibility for *our own health*—starting in our own kitchens and at our own tables. When we understand this complex problem we face together as a society, the path will become clearer. As a culture, we must choose to intentionally shop, cook, and eat better.

My experience as a Home Economics Foods teacher in middle and secondary schools in Vancouver gave me direct experience seeing the emerging problems with young people. The fast-increasing sedentary behaviors—including obesity, overuse of screen time (leading to technology addictions), and the latest phenomenon of vaping and e-cigarettes—are all quickly becoming major concerns. The major fallouts of all of these trends is the rampant increase in anxiety and depression in schools.

I taught a Foods Exploratory class in middle school, Grades 6-8, for five years. In the middle school, I saw each student nearly every day. I experienced how easily kids absorbed learning about food, cooking, and making healthy overall food choices. When we know better, we do better. They were inspired. Many mothers expressed how surprised and pleased they were when their children came home to cook, bake, and even clean up properly after themselves. Many children also loved learning about plants and gardening. They were fascinated while watching plants grow from seeds to salads on the table. Each year, more complicated methods and ingredients were added to our repertoire, as we incorporated BC's new inquiry curriculum into the process of Foods Exploratory classes.

As a result, the recipes included in this book were gathered and developed while teaching these 10- to 14-year-olds at Norma Rose Point Middle School. Students made all of these recipes and more, which means that if they can do it, you definitely can! These basic yet essential recipes round out the full plan for healing our guts as well as resetting our personal and family microbiome. If we follow basic guidelines in feeding our microbiome properly, this in turn will encourage us to make choices that are inherently good environmental choices that support healing of each microbiome and biome, up and down the food chain, thus helping to heal the planet. Each good choice we make will help restore the soil, air, and water. All of this can happen through what and how we eat as individuals and families.

The recipes included herein represent a start to incorporate basic healing and fermented foods and increase fiber into our day-to-day life. These include ideas to make weekday food preparation quick and easy, with a focus on foods that are easy to make and eat and are "lunch-kit friendly," for children and adults alike. This approach to lunches, in particular, was important to address in this book. Many people, both children and adults, leave home in the morning every day with high anxiety and stress-related symptoms. Often, extremely anxious individuals, when questioned by the school counselor about what they ate for lunch, for example, described their meal as usually not a picture of health. The number of juice boxes, Gatorade bottles, energy bars, and cookies consumed for convenience at lunch is astounding, to the detriment of everyone's mental health. It is time to stop buying flats of processed foods for lunches and get children involved in making their own, as a regular practice. Although this book is not an extensive recipe book, some ideas will get you started for creating a foundation for success. If you get your children involved in creating their own meals, they will feel more sense of ownership and a responsibility for their own health. It is fun for everyone when children are involved in the process.

We, as a society, truly need to intentionally move in this healthful direction. We already know it intrinsically, and we have to start somewhere. This is how to start where it matters most—in our own homes, with our own children and parents. To move in this direction, to feed and care for your microbiome, we need to shop in the organic section of the supermarket, buy more local produce, support organic farmers, and grow some of our own food. All of that will make an incredible difference in our lives and health, which is truly what this moment and movement is about. I know all of this is not possible immediately, yet we can intend to move in this direction over time. Then, things will change.

If you or anyone you care about has issues with immunity, obesity, or mood/mental health, consider that—maybe for the first time—you can truly help the healing process by increasing the consumption of good, whole, healthy foods, including a variety of fermented foods and lots of vegetable fiber. You *can* boost your family's health through the care and feeding of your family's microbiome.

The food-mood connection begins with an interconnected scenario that leads to inflammation. We are introduced to the idea that proper nutrition and a reduction of chemical intake supports the health of our microbial population. The health of our microbes prevents inflammation in our bloodstream, which effects our brain health.

Chapter 1—Key Highlights:

1. The human gut microbiome is a major component of human health.

2. The microbiome is instrumental in processing, absorbing, and utilizing the chemical and nutritional components of food at the cellular level. Since we have co-evolved with these microbes, they are essential for all aspects of human health.

3. Without these microbes and other essential nutrients, inflammation develops, which can precipitate a multitude of diseases.

4. We can assist various aspects of our health by mindfully supporting certain food-growing methods and consuming certain foods to support a proliferation of gut microbes.

Chapter 2: My Personal Story

My younger childhood was quite idyllic. I grew up on the clear and clean waterfront of Vancouver, BC, right on the beach. In Deep Cove, North Vancouver, we had the cleanest water to drink and to swim in. We ate fresh seafood, caught off our own wharf and beaches: small fish and even salmon, crab, clams, and mussels. This idyllic life is still possible today, in British Columbia.

My dad grew up in Vancouver during the Great Depression, raised in a house with a garden. He knew how to tend the plants and care for chickens and rabbits. His parents always had healthy organic food, right in their backyard. Because of my dad's childhood, my family of origin ate a lot of vegetables daily. They always had tomatoes growing outside. My mother lived more of a city life, but she always cooked food from scratch when we were children, even when processed food became popular. I had a healthy diet in my childhood and got off to a good start in life.

In my teenage years, I developed serious acne. My mother was very concerned about it, so we went to the doctor. At that time, the trend was a new prescription product, tetracycline. This was my very first exposure to antibiotics, lasting about two years.

Upon reflection, that course of treatment was a major event in my life because it coincided with a start of consistent weight gain. We now know that taking those types of drugs kills off strains of microbes in our gut biome population and creates havoc in our systems, over time.

Despite being relatively active and on a sports team, my weight consistently increased throughout high school. Little did I know that my hormonal life was also affected through taking that drug. Throughout my entire life, I experienced very short menstrual cycles, which was different from those of my friends—although it was not something talked about much.

I married when I was in my late twenties. One night, during a ski lesson in 1982, I had a bad fall and tore the anterior cruciate ligament (ACL) in my left knee. Back then, the operation was a major invasive surgery. Major antibiotics were administered before, during, and after surgery.

Recovery was a long, twelve-month-plus process that involved a huge, hinged cast and major antibiotics—antibiotics that probably depleted or destroyed my entire bacterial colony, again. Not only did I take the surgical antibiotics, but after that joint surgery, I was advised to take antibiotics before every dentist visit for the rest of my life, due to the possibility of infection in the joint. Antibiotics twice a year, just to go to the dentist! (Update: Since 2019, dentists finally no longer recommend this.)

My job during my thirties and forties was a very high-stress, project-oriented, corporate job, which I held for sixteen years. Although I loved my job, received many accolades, and had great experiences, I worked very hard in a project-based, deadline-driven environment. We now know from research that chronic stress (meaning ongoing, consistent stress) plays a role in the health of our microbiome—and not a good one. During that period, I developed rough eczema skin patches on my elbows, and used a steroid cream on the problem—more poison. I continued to not eat much fat, (afraid of the calories) to keep my weight down. Subsequently, I also had another ACL accident and then reconstruction on my right knee, with, of course, more antibiotics.

During the 1980s, my husband and I were keen on starting a family. Over the course of almost ten years, we experienced many approaches to having a baby, both with medical intervention and other consultation. We suffered through three miscarriages and many disappointments. My hormones were definitely off, which was never addressed or even mentioned in the years of medical consultation, fertility interventions, and subsequent adoption possibilities. Ultimately, we did succeed in having a child together.

Over the 26 years of my relationship with my then husband, I had many surgeries (mostly knee—I lost count but six or more), a very serious sinus infection, a Caesarean section, two carpal-tunnel surgeries, two hip replacements, a knee replacement, and a ruptured appendix. The latter was the worst by far, because I contracted sepsis and nearly died. Each medical problem seemed to include major doses of antibiotics. I think that could be the root of my many health issues. We now know that each dose of antibiotics can eradicate many species of microbes. In the long term, this can result in a depletion and even extinction of certain strains in an individual. The absence of certain strains combined with a genetic predisposition is what is now believed to be the root of many diseases.

At the time of all of those conditions, when I made decisions to have surgical remedies for my arthritis and other issues, I had no idea of the long-term implications of such strong drugs. Of course, I trusted the doctors in the white coats with no doubt and total confidence. I certainly did not understand nor was I ever advised as to the effects of repeated antibiotic therapy, or what effect it would have on my overall long-term health, physical, mental, and emotional. It was never explained to me.

I now know that antibiotics made my hormonal system and menstrual cycle dysfunctional. Drugs probably killed off much of my gut microbiome many times and seriously affected my immunity as a result. The end of all of that was a major effect on my fertility (or infertility) and the foundation of an autoimmune disease that formed in my body: inflammation leading to serious arthritis.

Ironically, all the way along, I unknowingly ate a highly inflammatory diet (very high in gluten) as well. I was the main person responsible for our groceries, cooking, and overall diet. After all, I was the well-educated nutritionist, not to mention a very well-intentioned wife and mother!

Along that path, I also suffered from seemingly unrelated symptoms: long-term insomnia, weight gain, eczema, acne, anxiety and panic attacks, brain fog, and poor memory. To be fair, other life things contributed to this, such as my mother's long-term illness, my daughter's and husband's struggles with anxiety and depression, the focus I had on school (including learning about all of this and more), and the stress of a strained primary relationship with my attention no longer fully on my nuclear family.

Since that difficult time, I have learned considerably about the importance and significance of diet as well as the effects of antibiotics—not only on general physical health, but also how particular foods, drugs, and environmental chemicals affect the health of our gut microbiome.

From the journey of my own discovery and recovery comes the information shared in this book.

My many years of being unaware of the damage to my microbiome paved the way for disease not only for me, but also contributes to problems for developing children. We understand much more about how a mother's health during pregnancy is important—for fetal development—from a nutritional standpoint. The mother's microbiome also affects the growth and development of the baby in utero.

The vaginal microbiome inoculation is possibly the most important contributor to a child's future health, but it's not just the inoculation itself that is important. The environment there sheds a whole new light on the importance of full-term birth and nursing. The colony of vaginal microbes changes throughout pregnancy. At 40 weeks, it is meant to be at the ultimate stage to inoculate the newborn with the specific microbes that assist the infant in digesting food from outside their body.

After birth, the breast milk is meant to hold and provide specific microbes and food for the infant, which enables digestion of the first solid foods. If the baby is premature, so is the vaginal microbiome and the breast milk, which affects the long-term health of the infant, in both of those ways.

Because Caesarian section babies do not get that initial vaginal inoculation, their microbiome consists of a variety of tissue cells—skin cells and other airborne microbes from the operating room personnel. These days, with the vast increase in Caesarean births, this trend has poor lifetime health implications. Sometimes, forward-thinking physicians and midwives provide mother's vaginal microbe swabs on the faces of babies born by emergency C-section. Sometimes, not.

Before we dig right into *The Food-Mood Connection: A Holistic Approach to Understanding the Gut-Brain-Microbiome Relationship*, we will look at the Human Ecological Model and an organizational diagram that illustrates all of the factors contributing to human and ecological health, to show the interconnectedness and complex context. The food-mood connection begins in the vaginal canal of a healthy mother and a timely birth. Lifelong mood, immunity, and body weight are affected through the microbial inoculation and chemical interaction that begins at birth, which all can be influenced by environmental interjections and interactions throughout life.

Chapter 2—Key Highlights:

1. Seemingly unrelated health issues can be directly related through our gut health and the human gut microbiome.

2. Antibiotics kill microbes indiscriminately, which has lifelong implications from an unbalanced microbiome and sets the stage for ongoing, lifelong health issues.

3. Microbiome inoculation at birth sets the stage for lifelong health or chronic illness, primarily in either immunity, mental health, or obesity—or even all three areas.

Chapter 3: The Human Ecological Model

The Human Ecological Model is a model of an ecosystem that illustrates human health and wellness and its relationship to the health of all life and the planet. The individual human or "collective human" is at the centre. The model illustrates many levels of interconnection through our health, including our internal human health and our connections to the immediate (or near), and the far reaching (or distal) world around us.

The concept of the Human Ecological Model is best understood by using a diagram. Note that even though the lines are solid, every section is interconnected and porous. The lines are drawn only to clearly divide all the sections, but they do not exist in reality. Divisions are shown to visually convey these areas and concepts more clearly for understanding.

HUMAN ECOLOGY MODEL
FOR HUMAN HEALTH OVERVIEW

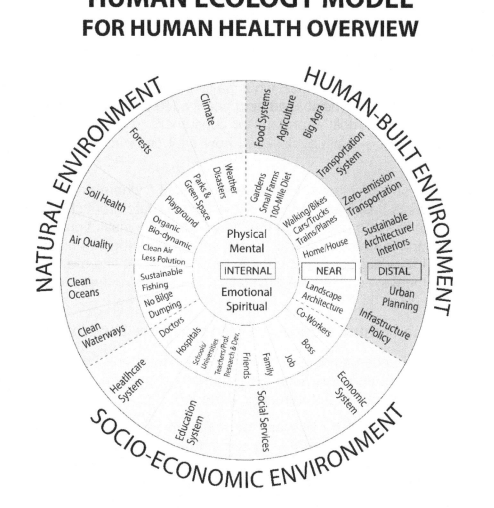

This model illustrates overall health from the human's perspective, at the core. As we move toward the outer ring, the environment within each circle is included in the next. The levels or concentric circles of environments are labelled *Internal Environment* (human, that is), the *Near Environment* (within reach or day-to-day) and the *Distal or Distant Environment*. For example, our human physical, mental, emotional, and spiritual health are discussed in the *Internal Environment*, or our basic individual level.

The pie chart further divides these environments using dotted lines, dividing the circles into these thirds: The *Natural Environment*, (just nature), the *Human-Built Environment* (man-made), and the *Socio-Economic Environment* (cultural), all which are factors in the three levels.

The diagram clarifies how important the connections and interactions of the "giant mobile" that is human health. It also illustrates how decisions made at all levels and how the sections of environment can affect the whole. Everything is interconnected and pushes or pulls on other areas, causing things to change. Human health is affected by "Agriculture and Pharmaceuticals" in the outside circle, through agriculture and health care in the Near Environment circle.

Depending on the governmental bodies that we live under in various countries and cultures, laws and policies cannot necessarily protect our health. When we have an educated social structure and those who make consumer decisions through solid knowledge, we can change society and our overall cultural health. Our culture is ruled by the economy, so it is most important for consumers to understand the power of their economic choices—at all levels—and how they can directly affect all of these environments.

This particular illustration shows the "Butterfly Effect," whereby we can see how change at the lowest, basic, and individual levels can create great change throughout the full system. In this approach (from the individual to the institutional level), we can see how the economic structure of society can and must be the means by which social change occurs. Individual consumer choice that is educated and motivated by health and wellness is the way to change policy, law, and social structure—one purchase at a time.

Interpreting the Human Ecological Model: Near Environment

For now, to gain an understanding of how this works, let's look first at an overview of the Near Environment and the Distal Environment. These are the two consecutive concentric circles outside of our Internal Environment.

The Near Environment is "up close and personal" to us. What we experience on a daily basis is our Near Environment—we see it, feel it, taste it, smell it, feed it, eat it, and/or live and sleep with it. Things such as food, clothing, and shelter comprise our near environment, as it is a study of our day-to-day life. More detail and explanations of all the categories in the diagram will be discussed in later chapters.

Interpreting the Human Ecological Model: Distal Environment

The Distal Environment, sometimes called the Distant Environment, consists of our connections to the overarching systems in the world and society that affect us: institutions, government, agricultural and food systems, laws, etc. The Distal Environment contains expressions of our national policies, at the highest levels. We are connected to them, even if we don't see them. The distal connections are through the states of our natural environment—from water coming out of the tap to weather and war—and includes the human-built versions of infrastructure as well as their ideas, at their core. All these things, at every level, affect our lives and our health—as you can see from looking around the circles. Distal relationships are not quite as obvious as the closer ones in our Near Environment, but they form the context and infrastructure in which the near interconnections form and shape the culture and our overall health.

Interpreting the Human Ecological Model: Internal Human Environment

Our Internal Environment is usually thought of in terms of multiple aspects: physical, mental, emotional, and spiritual health. Typically, when we talk about health, most people default to assuming we mean physical health. Fortunately, nowadays, discussing mental and emotional health issues is no longer taboo. Spiritual health, however, is still a sensitive topic, largely due to historical meanings assigned to what spirituality is. In past decades, people have described themselves as "religious," but in today's world, many identify as "spiritual" and "not religious" when asked about their belief system(s). With the current stress and strain of all levels of life (humans, animal, and plant life), all levels and types of health are at stake.

This is a key point in the future of our society and our planet. Without a spiritual connection to all life and our planet, we do not have an equal stake in the process of change. If we think of the Earth as a source of resources and wealth, then it logically follows that we use it for profit and personal gain. That is the system we currently live under—resources are the basis of our economic model, with a focus on growth. That attitude is what has created the situation with climate change we are experiencing today.

As humans, we have an innate need to believe in something bigger than ourselves, which forms a spiritual connection to something. Whether we see that connection as our collective humankind, among all species and their interdependence with God or Universal Energy, knowing that we now have the fate of the planet in our human hands is an overwhelming responsibility.

As city-dwellers, many of us now have a weakened connection to nature and this spiritual basis, evident especially among youth who spend very little time outside, in raw nature. Having a spiritual connection plus a faith for change is essential for our species' survival. Some believe technology will save us, but we are very close to being too late with technology alone.

As you can see from the Human Ecological diagram, our relationships with the Distal Environment, the Near Environment, and the Internal Environment are under stress. The conflict between the way things are and the way things need to be are causing huge impact on the health of everything on our planet. This conflict stems from many sources, but the connection to human "progress" in the last 100 or so years has been devastating for all levels.

This conflict can largely be linked to our dependence on fossil fuels in our transportation, food, pharmaceutical, and fuel systems and the effect of ecological balance. The petroleum-dominant chemistry starts with the discovery of the combustion engine and developing gasoline. It progresses through to the creation of thousands of chemicals used for everything from war weapons to garden pest-killers (both plant and animal). We then progress to many cleaning chemicals of all sorts, culminating in a myriad of cleaning, body, bath, and beauty products. As a result of all of these chemical components, humans have added so much toxicity to our water, air, and soil that the accumulation is having detrimental effects on all levels of life—including life at the smallest microbial levels.

Physically, our gut, lungs, and skin are our body's direct contact organs with the outside environment and the filters by which we, as organisms, divide ourselves from it. The gut lining and lungs are thus on the front lines through food, water, and air that we intake and need to survive. Adults alive today have endured decades of accumulation of a large variety of chemicals, through consumption of them through our food and water. In turn, the addition of petrochemicals causes degradation of natural resources. The increase of ingestion takes its toll on not just human bodies but all plants and animals, biome systems, and microsystems on Earth. Over time, the result is that all life is not operating at the most optimum levels. It is the massive load on these systems that leads to many of the health issues we experience not just in our human population, but throughout all systems on Earth. Our air, water, and soil health are seriously depleted, even though we cannot see much of it. It is piling up without relief and it accumulates in tissues until the tissues and related systems can no longer bear the load.

We now know that the foods our grandparents ate are much different from what we eat now. Fruits and vegetables, for example, do not carry nearly the same nutrients today as they did a hundred years ago. The vitamins and mineral levels we thought these foods contained have different nutrition tables now. A simple apple is no longer the same apple. Depleted soils, contaminated water, pesticide use, and chemical overuse have greatly reduced the nutritional assets of all the foods we eat. Internal integrity is greatly diminished in many plant and animal species all over the planet from this. Rapid extinction of many species is also a growing problem. It has been acknowledged by scientists that we are in the middle of the 6th great extinction on

Earth, which includes large mammals, such as elephants and whales, to which activists draw attention. It also includes the tiny life in microbial species that live in and on all surfaces of living things on the planet.

The current result is the "rainforest" that is our personal gut microbiome has now been under so much stress that the huge diversity that was our historical Internal Environment is now under tremendous threat. Many microbial species that have historically been common (still seen in people of some primitive tribes today), are under threat of extinction. This is largely due to our modern diet, which directly affects the diversity of the internal microbial community balance. When we reduce the diversity of that microbial community, we risk the possibility of dysbiosis, a condition enabling the "bad bugs" to outnumber the good ones, which can result in inflammation and then diseases, of all sorts. Particular foods have particular types of fiber which, when digested by the microbes, creates a particular chemistry that drives our immune system, our mental health, our ability to create and extract vitamins or minerals from our food, and our abilities to keep our hunger and weight in check.

Not only must we take more care with our interaction with the Near and Distant Environments, we need to take care of our Internal Environment as well. That's really what this book is about. Our microbiome is an underappreciated and largely unknown community which acts as an "organ," although it is not really an organ per se, but a community of "misfits." However, the resident and transient microbes that live within our bodies hold trillions of cells that work together to serve the human host. Ultimately, our microbes enable us to sustain a moist and warm environment in which to perpetuate their survival within us.

The Evolution of our Internal Environment

In the beginning of life on Earth, there were one-celled organisms. Lots of theories outline how those one-celled plant and animal creatures came to be on this planet and how they eventually evolved into the myriad of species that we see on Earth today.

The one-celled creatures are known as microorganisms or microbes. There are millions of varieties, consisting of bacteria, yeasts, fungi, protozoa, viruses, and more. They are literally everywhere—and have been, from the very beginning of life on Earth. They are still here, to this day. There are microbes in the air we breathe, in soil, and in the water vapour of clouds. In fact, there are microbes in all water, including rivers, oceans, lakes, streams, and puddles. There is even a community in a single drop of water.

Microbes live *in* and *on all living things.*

In recent times, microbes and other creatures have been discovered in very extreme environments, changing our beliefs about what life on Earth (and hence, other planets) might be able to tolerate. There are microbes at the bottom of the ocean, far from light, and microbes living in steam vents, at extremely high temperatures.

Living microbes are found in the upper reaches of our thin stratosphere, and have even been discovered on the windscreen of the space shuttle while in orbit! Some experiments in the Space Station have shown that microbes can live for months and even years, exposed to radiation and no atmosphere, while in and on the spacecraft labs. The Permaform Theory even suggests that life on Earth has been inoculated by passing and crashing comets and meteors that carry microbial life from far-reaching locations in our solar system or farther.

In mammals (we know mostly about mice, rats, and humans), according to the current science, *microbes live in and on all surfaces of our bodies*. We even have specific microbes that live on our skin, which may be quite different than those on our eyes or in our nasal cavities and mouth, different yet again from those varieties living in our gut. The largest concentration of these microbes is in our gut—the tube between our esophagus and our rectum—specifically, in our lower or large intestine. This is called our Human Gut Microbiome, or more commonly, the Microbiome, or Microbiota.

There are biomes and microbiomes, big and small, as previously mentioned, everywhere on the Earth, and possibly throughout the entire universe. The Human Gut Microbiome is specifically what we are concerned with in this book, as it affects our personal health so immensely. Much of this science has been brought to light in the last few years, but is certainly becoming mainstream and generally accepted among and between all of the medical and scientific professions.

The food-mood connection begins to emerge as a very small part of an overall planetary reliance on microbes. This interconnection of microbes is an integral part of life and health, at all levels.

Chapter 3—Key Highlights:

1. The Internal Environment is typically what humans consider their health and consists of a blend of mental, physical, emotional, and spiritual health.

2. Our Near Environment is our day-to-day life in the context of the ecological setting of the Natural, Human-Built, and Socio-Economic Environments, as shown in the Human Ecological diagram.

3. The Distal Environment is the entire and holistic context of how all of this fits into the overall ecology of human health—which fits in with institutions, and all systems as they exist on Earth, including all life and Human-Built Environments.

4. We have evolved from microbes and continue to have microbes *in and on all surfaces and organs of our bodies*. In fact, all levels of life on the planet have microbes—from the ocean depths to the upper atmosphere, as well as the air, soil, and water bodies in between. All life is covered and symbiotic with microbes, presumptively in the same way we are—co-dependent and symbiotically. Each organism NEEDS the others, to both survive and thrive.

5. All environments are interconnected and interdependent. They are also all in a fine balance, which is why it is so important to be aware of taking care of all life on the planet—great and small, not just human life.

Chapter 4: The Gut—Our Second Brain

Until recently, it was thought the brain and the developing human fetus were contained in sterile environments. It is now known that this is untrue, in both cases. Humans have microbes in and on *all* organs of our body. Our gut microbiome is unique in that it is a large population living together in our gut. This grouping seems to often function as a singular entity, giving us what we call a "gut feeling" or "gut instinct." We tell each other "it takes guts" when looking for fortitude in the face of fear. We have "butterflies in our stomach" when nervous. The individual microbes also function in particular chemical "waterfalls" at the cellular level as well as the organ system level.[3]

This human microbiome community of ours consists of approximately 1-3 kg of microbes (in an adult). That is definitely quite a large mass to go undetected for so long, but as a seemingly nondescript loose collection of microbes, it has been overlooked and essentially ignored. It is truly amazing that it is such a large part of the operation of our body. Likely, all living creatures and probably all plants have their own microbiomes; it would make so much sense, based on the research to date. We already have some data on domestic animals, and we are now studying the effects of the soil microbiomes on plants, from nutrient extraction to communication between organisms.[4]

Until just recently, it was thought that humans and all mammals were sterile with respect to our uterine beginnings. We do not initiate our personal collection of microbes until the magic moment when we emerge from the womb. This gathering of microbes grows and evolves with us throughout our lifetime, as a symbiotic member of our individual human conglomerate community. In fact, this community contains more DNA in the ten times more cells that the community includes, over the amount of DNA that a single human being owns. If you have heard this figure quoted in the press, it is actually true. We may have half as many numbers of cells in our body as our gut microbiome, and it is thought that there may the same to ten times more DNA from them than is expressed in those cells. Each microbiome is unique, although it appears that families share similar colonies, especially when living together. It seems that children raised with lots of animals, such as on farms or in Amish communities where studies have occurred, have their increased animal contact decrease their chance of allergies and food sensitivities. In those situations, it appears that some sort of natural "inoculation" is taking place.

The microbiome begins in the birth canal (for most of us), where our mother's vaginal environment, precisely timed to change to benefit the microbiome of the baby just before birth, inoculates the baby passing through. Then, breast milk composition is perfectly suited to grow and feed not only the infant, but also the microbiome! Breastfeeding is the only stage of life where humans don't have to eat fiber in order to ingest food for our microbes. The perfectly enhanced breast milk changes with different microbial cultures in the milk to prepare us for solid foods. Each stage of our young infant life and our relationship to our mother's body is intimately suited to our own personal growth and development—not just for ourselves, but also for our microbiome.

As we grow and evolve what we eat, our microbiome changes quickly with the change in our intake. It has been discovered that it takes only ten days of eating poorly to completely devastate the diverse population of the microbial community, and a full two weeks of eating properly again to restore it to the original population. As you can see from this simple example, the tendency in our cultural foodscape is to decrease the overall microbial diversity over time. We cannot continue to follow this trend because we really need that relationship. We are truly symbiotic with this community of DNA, as individuals and as a species.

Recent science has shown that there is *as much as 1 to 1.5 times more DNA* in the millions of our microbial DNA than our actual human DNA—but not as much as 10 times, which is often quoted in popular press![5.] This is difficult for us to wrap our minds around. As we humans begin to realize that we are more than what we appear to be, and the human part is not the whole organism, perhaps we can accept responsibility for feeding not just ourselves but our accompanying friends.

We are a community. Some speculate we may be just a "bag of human cells"— a host, in fact, carrying around a very large, very unique collection of these microorganisms. We supply a warm home for them, a safe place for them to be fed, protected, and reproduce, so they can be safely passed on, to our future generations. This is what we do, whether we know it, and whether we nurture it—or not.

Humans "Outsource" Cellular Functions to Microbes

It is now generally accepted that all life on Earth has evolved from microbes. Humans—in fact, all living things—probably evolved *around* these one-celled communities we now carry around. We have, over evolutionary time, "contracted out" a large variety of chemical cellular functions to these microbes. We are in the beginnings of research and we don't totally understand what this all means. We don't know yet what all the processes are—which part of us is really human, and which part is really the microbes.

Does this matter? Apparently, we all have very individual biomes. We know that when one particular thing works for one person, it doesn't necessarily work for another, because they both didn't start off at the same place, even if they live in the same household or yes, even if they are twins.

It also seems that human gut microbiomes "run in the family," since they are passed from mother to child, and from partner to partner through bodily fluids, touch, reproduction, and the like. Our pets also contribute to our microbiome. They have a major impact towards our immunity and overall health, including allergies to food and other allergic reactions.

From what we currently know, our microbiome is responsible for:

- our nutrient extraction, including vitamins and minerals
- our metabolism, with a huge effect on obesity, and many other diseases (including cancer)
- our immunity—meaning a lack of diversity or a microbiome in "dysbiosis" can be at the root of many diseases (autoimmune and more)
- our general mood and overall mental health, as well as specifics of diseases

From Birth

Our microbiome is given to us through the vaginal canal as an inoculation at birth. Before birth, we are in a fully sterile uterine environment (although this is now showing signs of change, in the research). The birth canal is stocked with a special blend of microbes (only present at the time of an expected, 40-week delivery date), which give the newborn a healthy start in life. This inoculation prepares us to be exposed to the environmental onslaught that begins as soon as we emerge. Breast milk is a further support to our immunity. Full of fat, it is the perfect food in preparation for the over-stimulation our brain and bodies encounter in our first few months of life outside the womb.

It is now known that once we get this premier inoculation at birth, it changes throughout our life cycle. It changes when we start eating solid foods. It changes when we eat meat and other proteins. It changes all of the time, depending on what we put in our mouths.

Rise of Caesarean Sections

The many babies born now from Caesarean section miss out on this very important inoculation, unless they are attended by forward-thinking and knowledgeable delivery room staff. C-section babies not exposed to a "vaginal swab" may have their own personal microbiome inoculation formed from the various delivery room staff and their skin cells, among other common varieties floating around the operating room. Missing this very first step can often cause major difficulty for the individual later in life, including a propensity for colic, asthma, allergies, a variety of mental health issues, immunity problems, obesity, and eating disorders.

Co-Dependence and Functionality

The fact is, we cannot survive without our microbial friends, and yet that is what we have created through chemicals (especially petroleum products) and our disconnection from nature in modern society. The fact that we already have this codependence with the microbiome and are not yet knowledgeable about its structure and function is one of the major scientific riddles of our time. Something this important requires serious further investigation. The good news is that it is attracting a huge amount of very talented, scientific study. We know much more now than even five years ago, and research is picking up speed. There are gut-brain connection and microbiome articles published regularly in popular newspapers and magazines, as well as in countless medical and scientific journals and textbooks.

Some of the biggest questions on this topic worth considering regarding the microbiome are:

1. What is really happening in this second brain?
2. How is it that everyone is so different in their reactions?
3. Who is in control, anyway?

These questions really remind me of Michael Pollan's book, *The Botany of Desire: A Plant's-Eye View of the World*.[6] This curious book is written from the plant's perspective, which is unusual. We humans are so egotistical to think mostly in our terms of the world and how it works—for us in particular.

In the book, *The Botany of Desire*, Pollan observes the common manicured lawn; cut grass we plant around our homes, parks, sports fields, golf courses, boulevards, and more. Manicured lawns migrated to North America from the rich courts of Europe 200-300 years ago. They are still seen as a status symbol of wealth. Lawns have taken over the yards and people of North America, even today, where they need artificial turf or watering systems to survive! We don't even realize it, but grass has us positioned as slaves to their growth, development, grooming, and reproduction.

Grass no longer needs birds and other animals to spread seeds to maintain and proliferate the population of grass seed. We do it all for them, every Saturday, like clockwork. We plant or sod our lawns, water, cut, and propagate them. We make sure they don't die, by using our very own precious water!

Just like we value a living thing like a plant or a lawn, our individual human gut microbiomes are *our* internal lawn or garden. It is time for us to all learn to nurture and feed it.

Our microbiome is essential to our survival—as individuals, but also as a species. Because we are probably not the only organisms on Earth with our own unique microbiomes (this has not really even been brought up yet in the research), all life on Earth likely depends on their particular microbiomes, for the very same reasons.

The good news is that we are beginning to understand the importance of this symbiotic phenomenon. It is under our control, if we want it to be.

However, we must band together as a society, to start making drastic changes to how we exemplify our values as a society and as a culture.

How much do we value life and health of all things, over profits—or how sweet or salty it tastes? We must show how we value life and our interdependence with all other organisms. We really must.

Human Genome and American Gut Projects

The Human Genome Project (HGP) was an international research effort to determine the sequence of the human genome and identify the genes that it contains. The HGP was coordinated by the National Institutes of Health (NIH) and the U.S. Department of Energy. Additional contributors included universities across the United States and international partners in the United Kingdom, France, Germany, Japan, and China. The Human Genome Project formally began in 1990 and was completed in 2003, two years ahead of its original schedule.

The work of the Human Genome Project has allowed researchers to begin to understand the blueprint for building a person. As researchers learn more about the functions of genes and proteins, this knowledge will have a major impact in the fields of medicine, biotechnology, and the life sciences.[7]

In 2003, when DNA was able to be analyzed for genetic composition from the work done on the Human Genome Project, scientists looked forward to the medical cures that could be discovered when the entire human genome was identified. It was believed at the time when we unravelled the human DNA sequences, we could analyze which gene performed exactly what function. It was believed in the beginning of the study that there was a gene or a genetic defect responsible for all disease and dysfunction of the human body and mind.

From this huge undertaking, it was truly thought that cures for many diseases were possible and predicted.

As it turned out, decoding the Human Genome did not attain this ultimate goal, although much was learned. Even though science determined certain genes triggered certain diseases, those genetic traits did not tell the whole story. It was discovered that individuals were "genetically predisposed" or that the possibility to develop a particular disease was in our genetic makeup. Not everyone develops those diseases they may have the genes for, however. Much was left uncovered and is still a mystery.

Ten years of research and millions of dollars were spent sequencing the entire human DNA genome, and we unravelled many details of the mystery. However, surprisingly, the Human Genome Project was not the miracle that was predicted. What resulted, following the lead of the HGP, was the start of the American Gut Project, which coincided with much of the early discoveries around the gut microbiome. Scientists knew something was up.

The American Gut Project was co-founded in November 2012, by Rob Knight, PhD; Jeff Leach, PhD; and Jack Gilbert, PhD; and was—and still is—a huge undertaking.[8] The American Gut Project is a crowdsourced, global, citizen science effort. The project, described May 2015 in *mSystems,*[9] is the largest published study to date of the human microbiome—the unique microbial communities that inhabit our bodies. This publication provided the largest public reference database of the human gut microbiome, which may help drive many future microbiome studies. What's more, according to the research team, the success of the American Gut Project validates citizen science as a practical model for engaging the public in research.

That research has made a great addition to the data collected for the Human Genome Project, including these clues for further research underway:

Diet—The number of plant types (therefore, fiber), in a person's diet plays a role in the diversity of his or her gut microbiome and the number of different types of bacteria living there.

Mental health—The team found that people with a mental disorder had more in common with other people with mental disorders, in terms of the bacteria makeup of their gut microbiomes, than they did with their mentally healthy peers.

The following videos are offered to readers, to give an overview of some of the first media I used in teaching about the Human Gut Microbiome. These are easily watchable and have lots of information for further research on the topic.

Ruairi Robertson's TED Talk: "Food for Thought" (still valid, as of May 2020).[10]

David Suzuki's *The Nature of Things: It Takes Guts*, Season 55, Episode 3 (still valid, as of May 2020).[11]

The food-mood connection deepens as we see how our food intake or "diet" can quickly change our microbiome, which can actually change our DNA. Yes, food can change our DNA. Our habits of eating directly affect our "second brain" (our microbiome). As research continues to occur, it shows that diet has a direct relationship to mental health.

Chapter 4—Key Highlights:

1. Our evolution has created symbiotic relationships between us and our collective microbiome.

2. The microbiome mimics an organ within our digestive tract as a "second brain."

3. How we are born and breastfed has a huge effect on our health over our lifespan because of our symbiotic relationship with our gut microbiome.

4. Our gut microbiome is the foundation of immunity, weight management, and mental health.

5. Without a balanced microbiome health, we are susceptible to a variety of diseases.

Chapter 5: The Human Gut Microbiome and its Role in Disease

It seems logical and prudent to discuss gut microbes next. They are, rightly so, the star of the show as well as this book.

The human gut microbiome begins at the birth inoculation and consists of a community of one-celled organisms. Depending on the health of the mother, the timing of the birth, and the kind of delivery, the inoculation determines the individual's health pathway throughout their lifespan. This group of microbes has been identified by some as our "second brain," as it speaks constantly with our brain through electrical impulses of the Vagus nerve (the longest and most complex of the cranial nerves) and the endocrine system, through hormonal chemicals.

Ancient cultures have always acknowledged this connection. It survives through our language and instincts. Having a "gut reaction" or "gut instinct" is really our mental emotional reaction that turns into physical feelings. That type of reaction often occurs through our subconscious, even though many of our reactions are based on environmental influences from other humans or animals or situations. Those reactions can be associated with body postures, facial expressions, smells, energy from others, suspicions, attractions, repulsions, and so on.

Much of our communication is non-verbal and occurs at subconscious and vibrational levels. Our microbes are part of this and the chemistry they produce can influence our emotions and behavior as well as our conscious thought processes.

The diagram on the opposite page helps to illustrate some of the most important physical functions of the gut microbiome:

1. Protection against pathogens

2. Synthesis of vitamins

3. Immune system development

4. Promotion of intestinal angiogenesis (the growth of new blood vessels).

5. Promotion of fat storage

6. SCFA production by fermentation of dietary fiber

7. Modulation of central nervous system

We will look at each of these in detail next.

THE VARIOUS FUNCTIONS OF YOUR GUT MICROBIOTA

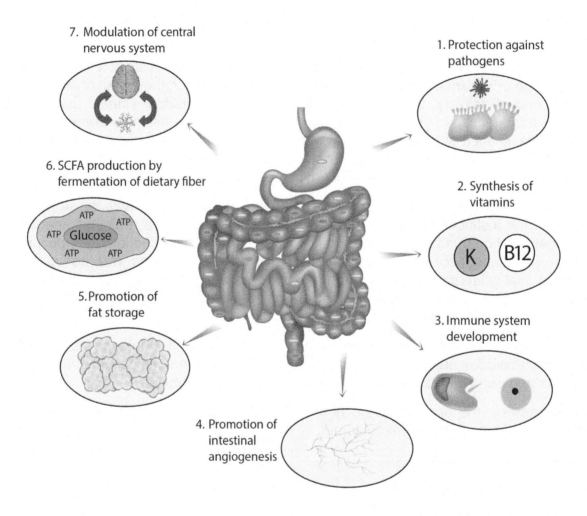

The diagram clearly identifies the seven major functions that the gut microbiota provides:

1. Protection against pathogens—Good bacteria, when they outnumber "bad bacteria," keep the community in check. The community will keep itself in check when fed and nurtured properly. When not in proper proportions of microbes (good vs. bad), the imbalance can cause dysfunction, which precipitates disease.

2. Synthesis of vitamins—Microbial life converts various products of intake into the vitamins that we cannot produce on our own. We must not only eat the food which contains the necessary nutrients, but we must also consume it and feed the microbes, which support the procession and extraction of the nutrients required.

3. Immune system development—Keeping viruses at bay and building up a resistance to invaders are key components of a good immune system. A healthy microbiome can resist disease in the gut, where diseases usually start. Our intestines are a giant filtration system that removes any unwanted pathogens or invaders. We must eat properly, to keep all of the cellular junctions in our entire gastrointestinal (GI) tract tight and wayward food particles out of the bloodstream. The leaking of food particles into our bloodstream is the basis of inflammation.

4. Promotion of intestinal angiogenesis (the growth of new blood vessels).

5. Promotion of fat storage—converts nutrients into smaller molecules for storage around the body which promotes obesity during dysbiosis or unbalanced microbial counts in the gut. For example certain strains of microbes regulate fat storage and if not in balance will over store, resulting in obesity.

6. SCFA production by fermentation of dietary fiber—SCFAs (Short-Chain Fatty Acids) are the main energy source of colonocytes (epithelial cells of the colon), making them crucial to gastrointestinal health.

7. Modulation of central nervous system—This is the ability to send and receive messages through chemical production.

All of these described functions work together through the cooperation of the microbial community. If the various players do not have a proper balance, then a state of dysbiosis (imbalance) is reached. That is when the early signs and symptoms of various diseases can begin to manifest. When we reach dysbiosis in our gut microbiome, the disproportion of certain players causes the chemistry in our bodies to be "off."

The microbiome has an important role in the maintenance of the gelatinous protective lining of the gut, so when the gel layer is thinned or when gaps occur, minor tearing of the one-cell thick intestinal walls can follow. This frequently develops into larger holes in the protective mucous layer as well as more tearing. Ultimately, this results in inflammation from particles of food leaching into our bloodstream through the leaks. This condition has become known as Leaky Gut Syndrome (LGS) and will be discussed in detail shortly.

The inflammation first occurs in the bloodstream, but it can travel anywhere and everywhere in the body. When we have a leaky gut, we have the potential to develop symptoms of disease *anywhere* in our bodies. This is key to understanding that the many symptoms that can present in our body from inflammation—seemingly unrelated, although they are definitely related through this gut weakness.

Inflammation is known to be the underlying cause of a multitude of diseases, possibly most diseases, and maybe even all. Certainly, there are genetic predispositions for every disease, but these predispositions do not necessarily decide who gets a disease and who doesn't.

Many people can have a certain gene but don't get the disease. Our bodies have an amazing capacity to prevent disease and to heal—if nurtured properly and allowed.

None of us is perfect. We are all only human! Our inherent genetic predisposition for certain diseases is our personal and unique "Achilles heel." For example, whatever our weak point in our body from genetic heritage is, it can play a role in our vulnerability.

However, this isn't the bottom line.

Having a genetic disposition is only part of the equation. That's why there is a lot of promise in the potential for improvements in human health in the future, using the knowledge of the functions of a healthy gut microbiome.

At this point in time, we are still not entirely clear on exactly what that looks like.

Our genetic predisposition can direct inflammation to our joints, to create arthritis; to our gut, to create irritable bowel syndrome (IBS), Crohn's disease, and colon cancer; and to our brain. Brain diseases related to dysbiosis in the gut include ADD (attention deficit disorder), ADHD (attention deficit hyperactivity disorder), anxiety, depression, Autism, multiple sclerosis (MS), Alzheimer's, and Parkinson's. We can have a genetic vulnerability to these diseases, but if we tend to our microbiome, we won't necessarily get the disease. If we do, we can help hold it in remission or prevent a full-blown expression of it.

At this point, it appears that many diseases can possibly be prevented and even treated simply by tending to our gut! This is being shown through a variety of research projects and programs around the world and there is much currently in progress. For example, there is now growing evidence of a direct connection between Autism and the gut microbiome. As high as 90% of autistic patients have gut disorders—in contrast to about 25% of typical children. Researchers reported the unpublished results at the 2019 International Society for Autism Research annual meeting in Montreal.[12]

Thomas Challman, medical director of Geisinger's Autism & Developmental Medicine Institute (ADMI) in Lewisburg, Pennsylvania, presented estimates of the prevalence of digestive problems in children with Autism, noting that they have varied widely, ranging from 9% to more than 90%. The new analysis is the largest yet of its type: it involves nearly 47,000 children, including more than 7,000 with Autism.[13]

Antibiotics, Prebiotics, and Probiotics

You have probably heard of these three terms, but in case you haven't or don't understand entirely what they mean, let's discuss them. Since you probably know what antibiotics are (and likely have some experience with them), let's start there.

Antibiotics

Antibiotics are, by definition, *anti* = against or opposing, and *biotic* = biological. So, against biology or life. Sometimes, the term *antibiotic* is broadly used to refer to any substance used against microbes. In the usual medical usage, antibiotics (such as penicillin) are those produced naturally (by one microorganism fighting another), whereas non-antibiotic antibacterials (such as antiseptics) are fully synthetic. Both classes have the same goal of killing or preventing the growth of microorganisms, and both are included in antimicrobial chemotherapy. Antibacterials include antiseptic drugs, antibacterial soaps, and chemical disinfectants. Antibiotics are an important class of antibacterials and are used more specifically in medicine and often in livestock feed.

Antibiotics are compounds produced by bacteria and fungi, which are capable of killing or inhibiting competing microbial species. This phenomenon has long been known and it may explain why the ancient Egyptians, Chinese, Greeks, and Romans had the practice of applying a poultice of moldy bread (an old precursor to antibiotics) to infected wounds. It was not until 1928 that penicillin, the first true antibiotic, was discovered by Alexander Fleming, Professor of Bacteriology at St. Mary's Hospital, located in the United Kingdom, in London.[14]

Modern antibiotics—medically or synthetically produced—are of what we are mostly aware. Even though some of us still use Granny's "old wives' tales" and chicken broth to cure our ailments, not many of us use moldy bread to keep a wound from developing an infection. Antibiotics are used to *kill or prevent infectious bacteria*. Unfortunately, antibiotics kill good bacteria along with the bad.

Repeated use of antibiotics is like a "carpet-bomb" to our intestinal tract as a side effect of attacking the specific site of infection. There are no specifics with antibiotics as to which species are injured or annihilated. Each time these drugs are administered to us, another or several species of good bacteria could be completely eradicated from our Internal Environment. For those of us who have had several surgeries, repeatedly use antibiotics pharmaceutically, utilize antiseptic cleaners on a regular basis, and/or eat foods with pesticides still on them, we need to know that all of these things kill bacteria outside *and* inside our bodies—indiscriminately. That is why it is so important to move towards eating organically and even consume biodynamic foods—to remove chemicals from our diet—and to remove chemicals as much as possible from our households, in all areas. This includes not just food, but laundry, kitchen and bathroom cleaners, pet care, cosmetics, and anything else we ingest or that comes into contact with our skin. This means that we, as consumers, now need to vote with our dollars to reduce the amount of antibiotics and other chemicals used in our entire food system.

Surely no one is against antibiotics, in principle! These drugs have revolutionized the health of the human race and enabled the eradication of many diseases or death sentences from simple infections. However, they have been grossly overused unnecessarily and consumers still are not properly educated in the use of them. Supporting *organic* and *biodynamic* farming (leaving the soil the same or better than when the crop started) is the only way to eliminate the overuse of chemicals in food. Leaving the decision to the producers has not seemed to work on the larger company producers.

Antibiotics are now in our water systems. They are in our drinking water, our rivers, and our oceans. They kill important microbes on ALL BIOMES now, and are endangering the extinction of all species. Let us remind each other that antibiotics kill everything indiscriminately—they are "carpet-bombs" everywhere, annihilating our microbes (both friend and foe microbes)—and we need our microbial friends very much!

Probiotics

The Food and Agriculture Organization (FAO) of the United Nations and the World Health Organization (WHO) define probiotics as "live organisms which, when administered in adequate amounts, confer a health benefit on the host." This was taken from the FAO website, in an article called "Probiotics in Food: Health and Nutritional Properties and Guidelines for Evaluation."[15]

Every true probiotic, whether consumed in food form (as in commercial or homemade yogurt, kefir, pickled vegetables, or condiments) or in supplement form (taken as pills, oils, or other) must consist of a known bacterial strain or strains, and must also have adequate scientific evidence backing up its health effects.[16] Known probiotic strains are *Bifidobacterium lactis*, *Lactobacillus acidophilus*, and *Streptococcus thermophilus*. These potentially provide health benefits and are commonly found in traditional, cultural, and ethnic foods, as well as in many in areas of the world where healthy longevity is studied and known.

Originally thought to have primarily gut improvements such as reducing abdominal pain in IBS, diarrhea, constipation, and the like, probiotics are under continuing further study and results in these areas are still forthcoming. Not only limited to gut health, it seems that the lack of mucosal gut barrier and the resulting leaky gut is related to many afflictions, including immunity and mood or brain health.

Through a study performed by Dr. Emeran Mayer, (a professor of Medicine, Physiology, and Psychiatry at UCLA), women who ate a high-microbe-count plain probiotic yogurt, for over four weeks, compared to a control group with no probiotics, showed remarkable results.

"What we eat can alter the composition and products of the gut flora—in particular, people with high-vegetable, fiber-based diets have a different composition of their microbiota, or gut environment, than people who eat the more typical Western diet that is high in fat and carbohydrates… Now, we know that this has an effect not only on the metabolism, but it also affects brain function… The fact that changes in our gut affect our brain's response to negativity or emotionally stirring images is mind-boggling… It means that what we put in our mouths and how we feed our gut bacteria do, indeed, affect our brain's functionality."[17]

There is also evidence that certain microbe strains may be specifically suited to some particular ailments. Recent research indicates probiotics may help reduce crying in babies who have colic and reduce cold and flu symptoms by supporting the immune system. There is also promise for eczema being treated with probiotics. Just think about that for a second—skin[18] conditions, colds[19] and flus, and colic[20] are all related to dysfunction in the gut! What? Yes, it is absolutely true.

Looking for the Right Probiotics

Many good quality probiotics are listed on the probiotic chart website.[21] (This site is actually a practice tool to assist with clinical decision-making for appropriate probiotic therapy.) Each probiotic should be described by a genus and species name, followed by a strain designation. Most products have shown relief for diarrhea and constipation. One product noticed on the list was CalmBiotic™, which contains strains of *Bifidobacterium longum R0175* and *Lactobacillus helveticus R0052*. This product was shown to improve both mood and affect (poor levels of each are symptoms of stress and anxiety), although it should not be used a substitute for standard treatment. (Note that the annotations are not in contradiction to any doctor-recommended medications, or internal or topical applications.)

Experimental results are not dependable or consistent, however, so it appears that the starting point of the health of the gut may drastically affect the results of a probiotic on a particular patient and their particular microbiome makeup at the introduction to it.

Not all probiotics are the same, so when you are choosing a probiotic, look for the one that has been studied for the specific health benefits you need. When looking for quality probiotic products to buy in the marketplace, choose those that contain at least the following species:

Lactobacillus plantarum—Found in kimchi, sauerkraut, and other pickled or fermented vegetables, this is one of the most beneficial bacteria in the body.

- It survives in stomach for a long time. Other strains can be susceptible to stomach acids and need gelatin capsules to bypass the stomach.
- It helps regulate immunity and control inflammation in the gut.
- It helps prevent disease, as it maintains the right balance to stave off rogue colonies.

- It fortifies the gut lining, repairs the intestinal wall, reduces gut permeability, prevents food allergies, reduces inflammatory responses, and absorbs and maintains levels of important nutrients such as Omega-3 fatty acids, vitamins, and antioxidants.
- It is essential for fighting infection as well as controlling inflammation and pathogenic bacteria.

Lactobacillus acidophilus—This is the darling of fermented milk products, including yogurt and kefir.

- It aids immune system by balancing good and bad bacteria.
- It helps curb the growth of Candida albicans (which causes yeast and other infections).
- It helps control cholesterol levels.
- It produces many substances that combat pathogenic microbes, including acidophilin, acidolin, bacteriocin, and lactocin.
- It manufactures lactase (which is needed to digest milk) and vitamin K (which promotes healthy coagulation of blood).

Lactobacillus brevis—Sauerkraut and pickles owe a lot of their benefits to this bug, which improves immune function.

- It combats vaginosis and also inhibits effects of certain gut pathogens.
- It increases levels of the all-star, brain-growth hormone called the BDNF (brain-derived neurotrophic factor).

Bifidobacterium lactis—This is found in fermented milk products, such as yogurt.

- It prevents digestive ailments and boosts immunity.
- It knocks out foodborne pathogens, such as salmonella (which causes diarrhea).

Bifidobacterium Longum—This is one of the first bugs to colonize our bodies at birth and can be found in many food types, including yogurt, kefir, seaweed, and miso soup.

- It improves lactose intolerance and prevents diarrhea, food allergies, and the proliferation of pathogens.
- It reduces anxiety and maintains healthy cholesterol levels. It can help reduce the incidence of cancer by suppressing cancerous growths in the colon. It can also help prevent colon cancer by effectively lowering the intestinal pH level.

Prebiotics

Prebiotics are essential foods for the beneficial microbes who live on us and in us. Most prebiotics are dietary fibers (but not all dietary fibers are prebiotics). Prebiotics, being high in fiber, are not digestible by humans, so we actually *need* the help of microbes to digest them for us. As a result, we humans have developed this symbiotic relationship, *over a very long period of time*. No one knows when this developed, but it is speculated that when man harnessed fire and developed the cooking of food, we began, through food, to change our DNA. We were able to more easily break down the structure of foods, when cooked.[22] We were able to spend less time hunting, gathering, and eating—and more time observing and trying new behaviors, which developed our brain size and power. In the end, these microbes are able to produce essential nutrients from what we eat. We now know we need the microbes to do so because, over time, we have lost the ability to do these tasks ourselves.

Prebiotics, commonly known as various types of plant-based fiber, provide health benefits by specifically altering either the composition or function of the gut microbiota through feeding our probiotic friends. Humans cannot digest prebiotics—but certain beneficial microbes can! Prebiotics may increase levels of beneficial bacteria, depending on the particular plant fiber. Prebiotics may also increase microbe-derived metabolites (signaling molecules), which are important for health. (For example, they are the communicators between the gut and the brain, and will be discussed in other sections of this book.)

Resident microbes (ones that stay in your gut) and transient gut microbes (ones that move through and are eliminated) can produce beneficial compounds (for example, short-chain fatty acids) from the utilization of prebiotics. Both resident and transient microbes promote a healthy gut—and in doing so, affect the overall health of the organism by contributing to cellular and system chemistry.

In more technical terms, a prebiotic is a substance that is selectively utilized by host's microorganisms providing a health benefit. Health benefits of prebiotics can be but are not limited to[23]:

- Improving mineral absorption
- Modulating the immune system
- Modulating satiety
- Improving bowel habits (reducing occasional constipation and diarrhea)
- Promoting metabolic health
- Improving symptoms of IBS
- Reducing risks of allergies of all sorts
- Supporting energy balance and glucose metabolism

Whole fiber improves blood lipids and blood glucose regulation. Some prebiotics can be found in onions, garlic, unripe bananas, chicory root, and Jerusalem artichokes. Low amounts of prebiotics are also available in whole grains, as well as in cruciferous and leafy green vegetables. In order to take advantage of the higher-fiber prebiotics, eating lower amounts of root vegetables and fruits is advised because of the higher sugar storage in root vegetables. Also, aim to reduce the overall sugar in your diet, for optimum performance of all organs and systems, particularly the brain.

Read labels when shopping for any processed foods. Look for these particular ingredients on labels to properly identify the various types of fiber:

- Galactooligosaccharides (GOS)
- Fructooligosaccharides (FOS)
- Oligofructose (OF)
- Chicory root
- Inulin

In order to increase the amount of prebiotic fiber in our diets, eating vegetables that have the highest fiber density is recommended—including cruciferous vegetables, such as broccoli, cauliflower, Brussels sprouts, and cabbage.

More higher-fiber vegetables include celery, artichokes, asparagus, Jerusalem artichokes ("Sunchokes"), onions, and garlic. Also included in this high-fiber list are leafy greens such as arugula, kale, chard, spinach, and various lettuces.

The Antibiotics-Probiotics-Prebiotics Cycle

After reading the previous section on antibiotics, probiotics, and prebiotics, you will understand details about each independently.

However, there is an important cyclical relationship between antibiotics, probiotics, and prebiotics. If we use antibiotic or antiseptic products that are so commonly used in our society, it is very important to be aware of this interdependency.

The diagram on the opposite page illustrates how antibiotics destroy microbes, and that the probiotics and prebiotics can repopulate the community.

Take some time to look at this diagram carefully, before you move onto the next section.

ANTIBIOTICS-PROBIOTICS-PREBIOTICS CYCLE

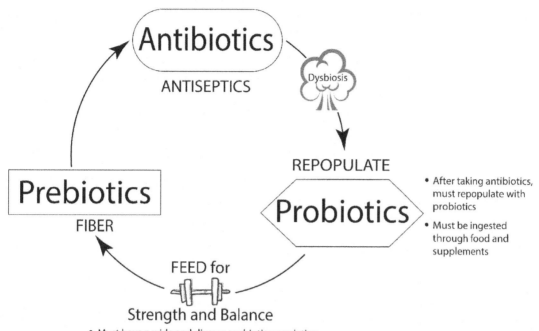

Dysbiosis

Going forward as a society, it is imperative we improve our eating habits, for many reasons previously discussed. Otherwise, we are all going to suffer more, from various diseases and other health problems, including dysbiosis.

Dysbiosis is a disruption in the microbiome, such as from treatment with antibiotics. Symptoms of dysbiosis can be from SIBO (Small Intestinal Bacterial Overgrowth), which can include every organ along the "tube" (your digestive tract, also called the GI tract)—your mouth, throat, esophagus, stomach, small intestine, large intestine, and anus. This disruption can present itself via a wide variety of symptoms, such as acid reflux or heartburn, loss of appetite, nausea, or abdominal pain (due to excess gas produced from fermentation in the upper intestine). It can also include fever, watery diarrhea, constipation, or cramping.

Dysbiosis can also lead to Leaky Gut Syndrome (LGS). Causes of LGS vary, but the most important is dysbiosis (an imbalance in the bacteria in the gut microbiome). Dysbiosis can occur from too much bad bacteria (such as an overgrowth of *harmful* bacteria, yeast, or parasites), or not enough *good* bacteria. Dysbiosis is commonly caused by poor diet, a course of antibiotics, using chemicals in cleaning supplies or in gardening, frequent use of antacids (or other over-the-counter drugs), and stress. Sometimes, even when you have enough good guys in the "room," they go along with the bad guys because of other factors. This is akin to having a bad crowd in a classroom; it changes the local culture and the bunch follows the bad leader.

Gut bacteria are important because they interact with your immune system to keep it healthy, and they transform your eaten food into essential healthy compounds, especially short-chain fatty acids (from Omega-3 essential oils). These particles heal the tight junctions between gut lining cells and protect the integrity of the gut barrier. This is why eating a variety of foods is so important. The food you eat determines which bacteria thrives and which compounds are generated during digestion.

When we have porous lining in our intestinal tract, and a damaged mucous lining (from not eating enough cartilage and collagen), larger than normal molecules can access the bloodstream directly, causing a leaky gut and inflammation.

The following diagram, which was reproduced from a diagram originally found in Dr. Josh Axe's book called *Eat Dirt: Why Leaky Gut May Be the Root Cause of Your Health Problems and 5 Surprising Steps on How to Cure It* shows just how a leaky gut allows inflammation to occur in the bloodstream. The microbes shown in the diagram below occur in the inside of the GI tract. When the mucosal lining has gaps, various foods (mostly lectin) can attack and create gaps in the gut walls, allowing the microbes access to the bloodstream. This is how inflammation begins in the gut.

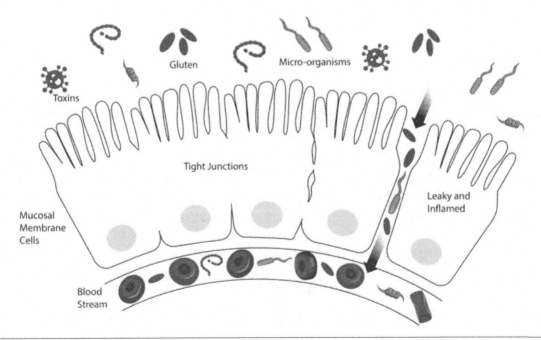

What, Exactly, is Leaky Gut Syndrome (LGS)?

What is a leaky gut, anyway? It sounds horrible! Many of us have heard this term used (it's been in the news), but we might not know what it means, so here is a very simple explanation of what it is.

Many of us think of the gut is just our stomach, but it is much more than that. It is the entire digestive tract—mouth, throat, esophagus, stomach, upper or small intestine/bowel, pancreas, liver, lower or large intestine/bowel, and anus. (Fun fact: If we took an individual's "guts" from their body and spread them out on the ground, they would cover about 200 meters, or the size of an entire tennis court!)

The food goes into our mouths at one end of the tube and the by-product is eliminated out the other. In between these two points, food interacts with the one-cell thick barrier that is known as "the gut." The emphasis on this organ to note here is that the entire thin tube after our stomach is only about one cell thick. This one-celled wall separates our food (and the organs processing it) from our bloodstream. Thus, it can be quite vulnerable if not correctly maintained.

Food is not supposed to actually touch the actual cells that form the organs along the route.

The whole tube is protected by a mucosal lining—at least, it is supposed to be—and muscles in the entire gastrointestinal system work together to form coordinated waves, moving food down from the mouth towards the end of the tube to the rectum. The tube should be lined with mucus to protect the walls from stomach acid. The surface of the intestines, where the extraction action occurs, is lined with little "finger-like projections" that stick out into the flow of liquefied foods. The projections are called villi and they greatly enhance the surface area and absorption capability of the bowel.

Throughout the length of the tube, those specialized tissues are essentially one cell thick and act like a giant filter. They represent one of the few barriers we have between the outside environment and our interior systems. In fact, the gut lining accounts for 70% of our immune system. The other filters are our lungs and our skin. Lungs are also only one cell thick, but our skin seems quite thick by comparison. These one-cell barriers are quite vulnerable to injury, and in the gut lining's case, when particles get through this one-celled layer, they have direct access to our blood supply. This is what can contribute to inflammation.

Even though we replace most of our cells quite often, the replacement cycles ranges from two or three days in our mouth and intestinal tract, and from one week to four months in our blood. Our bones, in contrast, are gradually replaced, cell by cell, about every seven to ten years! Other types of cells in our body remain with you for most of life, including your brain, which can grow back some parts and grows at the cellular level. Our eye lenses, for example, last for your entire life and do not replace themselves.

The gut tube cells are very adept at repair and replacement, so it is curious that this rate of cell repair is not enough to keep our gut from eventually leaking. The fact is that this organ is very good at regeneration, and it does a great job for a very long time. Because of this great job, many of us in the western world—eating a regular high-gluten, high-dairy, high-sugar, high-fat diet—typically have a leaky gut and don't even realize this is the case—at least, not in the beginning stages. Change can be very subtle and slow. It is not usually until symptoms get out of control that we start investigating the causes.

Leaky Gut Syndrome occurs through a long-term or consistent consumption of certain foods. These foods may not be harmful when eaten infrequently or in small quantities, such as gluten, for example. Let's follow gluten through the digestion process of a normal North American diet to see what can happen.

When we are young and we eat gluten, it is not usually a problem. Even if gluten creates a small tear in our gut lining, being young and healthy with frequent cell reproduction, we repair the damage straightaway. This starts out perhaps when we eat cereal for breakfast, creating a small damage that repairs itself. If we eat a sandwich for lunch, that's more wheat (and gluten), so the lining tears again and is repaired. If we have pasta for dinner, the same thing happens: damage and repair. When we eat food that is highly inflammatory, this goes on for days, weeks, months, and years. We can go on for years repairing the damage, but one day it catches up with us and the repairs are not complete. Food particles creep into the bloodstream and the inflammatory response process is initiated.

Here in the west, many eat a diet almost entirely of processed food. Except for a small percentage of the population, during a regular given week, working families (both parents work) often rely on frozen food, restaurants, and take-out. A modern working mother would feel quite virtuous coming home with a barbecued chicken and bagged salad for dinner, which is much healthier than the family eating fried chicken and French fries or pizza for dinner next door, or the pasta and the high-carbohydrate meals often served in typical cafeterias in institutions like schools, universities, and even hospitals.

Scientists from the American Gut Project have been monitoring microbiomes of many individuals for quite some time now. They have discovered that we literally *are what we eat*, just like Mom and Granny told us. Garbage in, garbage out. The microbes and thus our microbiome grow in diversity, shrink, and vary with the variety of foods we eat, often to our detriment. What we eat affects the population and diversity, but so does what we drink. Whether or not we exercise, smoke, or have high or chronic stress are also contributing factors that affect the population of the microbiome and its diversity of species. Additionally, if we are in a toxic environment and/or exposed to cleaning chemicals and/or antibiotics, that takes another toll. In these ways, the buildup of vulnerability increases, and inflammation increases, causing each individual's particular dilemma.

On the food front, the TV documentary *It Takes Guts* followed someone who lived solely on a McDonald's diet (consisting of Big Macs, Cokes, and Chicken McNuggets) for 10 days. After 10 days of this diet, the key subject's microbiome shrank to a much less (approximately 50% less) diversified version. To recover, it took more than 14 days of healthy eating to return to the previous microbial population numbers. This is an easy example of a losing battle: 10 days backward and 14 to recover. A June 2012 *Scientific American* article, written by Jennifer Ackerman, outlines dramatic changes to our microbial companions and the price we now have to pay for changing the culture of our gut through our high-carb, high-fat, and high-sugar diet, and the vast reduction in fiber.[24]

Our western diet, pharmaceutical overuse, and house-cleaning habits are exterminating species of microbes at an incredibly high rate—and this is just from conditions *inside the home*. The unfortunate thing is that most of this is completely uncalled for. For example, something as simple as hand-washing dishes is much more supportive of our immune system, building immunity through small samples of bacteria on a long-term basis. According to a Swedish study, the Huffington post reported that children who lived in households who hand-washed dishes in the kitchen sink were 40% less likely to develop allergies than those who used automatic dishwashers.[25]

Scientists tell us that we are in the midst of the 6th great extinction of the world's plant and animal population, especially those animals on the *danger of extinction* list. Yet very few write or speak about how this trend affects the unseen microbial population, because it is not just the big mammals that are in trouble, it's every living thing up and down the food chain, from the very smallest to the largest members. Similar to our current rate of extinction of species on the planet, we are exterminating our own health by unknowingly killing off our microbiome through bad food systems and diet. It's not good for us and it grows worse with every generation since ones from the 1950s.

Healthy eating consists of foods rich in fiber, collagen, and water, and consuming low-sugar, low-gluten, and other anti-inflammatory foods. By eating this way, the gut lining maintains a strong barrier to keep food particles out of the blood stream. When we don't have the right foods in our gut and the right balance of microbial life, dysbiosis develops and so does trouble.

If we eat a diet high in gluten, for example, over time, it will create havoc. Consider this typical day of my former life: a bowl of cereal for breakfast causes my gut lining to tear a bit, but my body repairs it. For lunch, I had a sandwich, tearing the lining again, which gets repaired. For dinner, I had pasta and a salad, causing more tearing, which my body repaired yet again.

Our bodies are strong, and if we eat healthily, we can repair the tears, for years and years. At some point, a full repair is no longer possible. We get particles of food in our bloodstream and our antibodies sense it and go on the warpath, gathering the white blood cells and causing inflammation. This inflammation is the bottom-line problem.

Once we have inflammation, we have the basis for disease to start. Once we have inflammation, at any point in our lives, we set the stage for a variety of diseases—in fact, some scientists say, all diseases.

What does all of this have to do with a "leaky gut"?

Before you develop a leaky gut, your immune system has a very clear job. The innate immune system is the body's first line of defense, allowing you to recover from injuries (such as a sprained ankle) or infections (such as the common cold). When you come into contact with a virus, your adaptive immunity "remembers" the bug and is able to figure it out fast, so at your next exposure, the system is prepared. This is true with all beneficial microbes from local, natural sources. This makes your system adaptable to your local surroundings and prepares you to eat in your local community area, from local farms, gardens, and such. With all the travel we do in modern times, our exposure is ever farther-reaching, and we are exposed through world-wide trade to more and more pathogens and insects/pests that travel along with the shipped foods. Everyone in the world has this ability to adjust and adapt to local foods, but this has been much more complicated with bacteria of all kinds from all over the world, travelling by air and sea, either with us, in us, or on us.

Once you have openings in the tight junctions of the intestinal lining (which contains 70% of your immune system), immunity is easily compromised. Zonulin is a protein that modulates the permeability of tight junctions between the cells of the wall of the digestive tract, and once zonulin keys the junctions to open, antigens can make their way through to the bloodstream, and this is where inflammation begins.[26]

Leaky Gut Syndrome is one of the major factors in nearly every inflammation condition. Inflammation is seen more and more to be at the root of diseases of all sorts. Chronic systemic inflammation of numerous illnesses are believed to have an autoimmune basis, and they are all linked to or caused by a leaky gut. This is not just a claim I am making. Research backs this up. According to research conducted on both animal and human subjects and published in journals such as *The Lancet,* a British medical journal, and the *International Journal of Gastroenterology*, it is suggested that LGS causes autoimmune diseases, and *Clinical Gastroenterology and Hepatology* and *The National Library of Medicine* have found that Leaky Gut Syndrome (or increased intestinal permeability) has been linked to the following symptoms and conditions:

- ALS[27]
- Alzheimer's[28]
- Anxiety and depression[29]
- ADHD[30]
- Autism[31]
- Candida[32]
- Celiac disease[33]

- Chronic fatigue syndrome[34]
- Crohn's disease[35]
- Fibromyalgia[36]
- Gas, bloating and digestive pain[37]
- Hashimoto's disease[38]
- IBS[39]
- Lupus[40]
- Metabolic syndrome[41]
- Migraine headaches[42]
- Multiple sclerosis[43]
- NAFLD (non-alcoholic fatty liver disease)[44]
- Parkinson's[45]
- Restless Legs Syndrome (RLS), Rheumatoid arthritis, and skin inflammation (eczema, psoriasis, rosacea, dermatitis, and acne)[46]
- Type 1 Diabetes[47]
- Type 2 Diabetes and Ulcerative Colitis (UC)[48]
- Various allergies and food sensitivities[49]

The interesting thing is that not all people who house the bad bacteria and the opportunity to develop the diseases do not ultimately get the disease(s). Common denominators underlie, but do not accurately predict the development of disease. Various factors set up the opportunity, but these three specific factors must all be present for the actual disease to result:

1. Genetic susceptibility
2. Exposure to inflammatory antigens (invading microbes or pathogens)
3. Damaged gut lining

The microbiome assists the immune system in healing the gut lining. Exercise also assists the microbiome to keep up populations of good guys in the gut. The critical species are the *Lactobacteria* that predominate the small intestine and the *Bifidobacteria* that predominate the large intestine. Humans depend on these organisms to absorb nutrients and fight against infection as well as feel satiety and keep us in a good mood. These organisms also support the mucous membranes of the gastrointestinal and reproductive tracts, the respiratory system, and the sinus cavities.

The other factor involved in the leaky gut phenomenon is the mucous lining of the intestines. This lining protects the epithelial cells (the one-cell thick wall which divides the intestinal contents from bloodstream).

An increase in access to the bloodstream by intestinal contents happens through the lessening and disappearance of the mucous lining of the individual's digestive system (the gut).

As the junctions between cells weaken, and the molecules of food and waste permeate the blood, a leaky gut occurs. This essential mucosal lining is created mostly from processing cartilage that is found in tendons, joints, and gristle of animal products. Cartilage consumption (which ingested through, long, slow, simmer-cooking of organic chicken and beef bones to dissolve marrow and cartilage to make bone broth) has decreased rapidly over the last fifty years. We consumers have been marketed more and more packaged meat, fish, and poultry products. Many people buy and eat meat and never ever see or touch a bone, cartilage, or gristle. Even fewer of us boil our bones to extract the cartilage that our bodies so desperately crave. The old tale of "chicken soup heals everything" has a lot of truth to it because the cartilage is the key to healing the joints between cells in the gut lining as well as the joints between our bones.

Improve Dietary Habits

There is now much concern—even at government levels—about the state of health and wellness in Canada's population. Concerns are rising about the skyrocketing collective costs of healthcare as the Baby Boom generation hits the age of retirement. Over the last few years, several countries have developed new guidelines for eating, to help educate the population on healthier eating habits. The fear in some countries, especially those which have government-sponsored healthcare systems, is that healthcare is becoming unsustainable in its current state. We need many varieties of disciplines of health practitioners to share the substantial load of need, but we also need individuals to *take charge of their own healthcare*. The way our system is currently set up is for *sick* care, not *health* care, and it is time individuals took back the reins. This means learning from an early age how food works in our bodies; how to plant, grow, cultivate, and harvest it; and how to store and cook healthy foods in sustainable ways.

Brazil's Dietary Guidelines

In 2014, Brazil published its dietary guidelines[50] aimed at all professionals working on health promotion and disease prevention. This included government and medical health professionals, nutrition and health educators in schools, and community and social workers. Brazil is still a developing country and its population experiences just as much poverty and under-nutrition as wealth and obesity. Using the guidelines, training and familiarization with groups of health professionals preceded the release of the plan to the public. These guidelines have subsequently become the "gold standard" throughout the world and have influenced Canada's Food Guide's recent update.[51]

The Brazilian guidelines read more like a Michael Pollan book (such as his book, *Food Rules: An Eater's Manual*, where Pollan advises to "Eat food, not too much, mostly plants") and are very different from the American MyPlate or the old U.S. Food Pyramid.[52]

The Brazilian guide focuses on the following "Ten Steps to Healthy Diets":[53]

1. Make natural or minimally processed foods the basis of your diet.
2. Use oils, fats, salt, and sugar in small amounts when seasoning and cooking natural or minimally-processed foods and to create culinary preparations.
3. Limit consumption of processed foods.
4. Avoid consumption of ultra-processed foods.
5. Eat regularly and carefully in appropriate environments and whenever possible, in company.
6. Shop in places that offer a variety of natural or minimally-processed foods.
7. Develop, exercise, and share cooking skills.
8. Plan your time to make food and eating important in your life.
9. Out of home, prefer places that serve freshly made meals.
10. Be wary of food advertising and marketing.

In this plan, the key ingredients to a healthy lifestyle are buying fresh and eating home-cooked food, increasing the cooking of food, avoiding processed foods of all sorts (including awareness around marketing influences), increasing the family and social aspects of food, and cooking and eating in social groups.

The U.S. plan continues to focus on food groups and less on the social and sustainable aspects of food. As a country whose values reflect economic choices (rather than health choices) around food—and where the food industry is largely lobbied in the process of government policy—the U.S. MyPlate guide starkly contrasts with the progressive Brazilian version.

Canada's Food Guide Update

Canada's Food Guide was updated in January 2019 after languishing since the last review with the rainbow of food groups in 2007.[54] The new Canadian Food Guide emulates the Brazilian guide more than the American ones (Food Pyramid or MyPlate), for the first time, in that it was written without food groups or recommended servings as in the past. Instead, the focus is on healthy eating, fresh food, and eating habits—rather than on food groups and the number of servings required per day.

Aside from the "plate" diagram, which illustrates the proportions of a healthy meal (one half of your plate being vegetables [with some fruits], one quarter being protein/meat, and the other quarter being whole grains), here are Canada's Food Guide's "Healthy Eating" guidelines:

Healthy eating is more than the foods you eat. It is also about where, when, why, and how you eat.

1. Be mindful of your eating habits.
2. Take time to eat.
3. Notice when you are hungry and when you are full.

4. Cook more often.
5. Plan what you eat.
6. Involve others in planning and preparing meals.
7. Enjoy your food.
8. Culture and food traditions can be a part of healthy eating.
9. Eat meals with others.

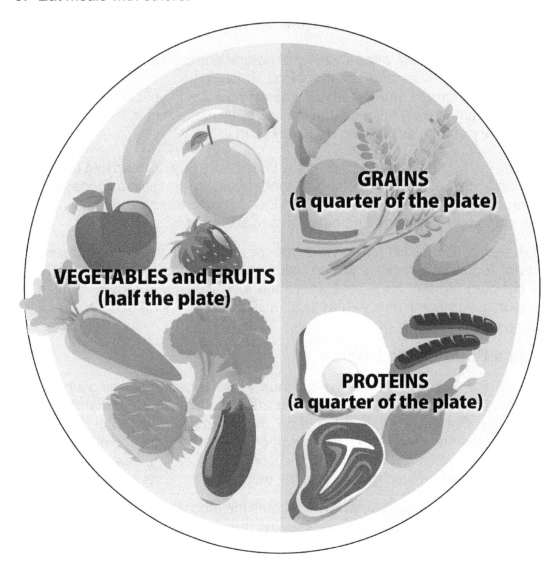

All of these steps and the new Canadian Food Guide are meant to encourage an increase of nutrient-rich foods and a decrease in processed, packaged foods. This is because of all of the added sugar (fructose, corn syrup, and many other words, which translate to SUGAR) in most processed foods—the real reason we must remember to read labels! A large variety of unhealthy fats (soybean, canola, and sunflower) are also added to most processed foods. Healthy fats (such as Omega-3s from fish oil and flax oil) are essential for our brain and heart health as well as many chemical cascade processes at the cellular level.

The Gut Microbiome Connection to Diseases Across the Lifespan

As mentioned in my introduction and personal story, the connection of the gut microbiome is becoming more and more proven. As far back as Greek and Roman times, a connection was drawn between the gut and disease. In fact, folkloric healing included many "prescriptions" from grandmothers for chicken bone broth and lemon tea with a good night's sleep, to cure many symptoms and ailments. Expressions such as "an apple a day keeps the doctor away" have been passed down for millennia, and it actually has been proven to be very truthful and beneficial to eat an apple a day, for a strong, general immunity![55] It has also now been proven that a poor vaginal inoculation of the microbial population can lead to a lifetime of poor immunity, mood issues, and a tendency to obesity—unless remedied.

Autoimmune Disease

One of the largest and fastest-growing groups of diseases we have in western society are those classified as an autoimmune disease. This includes Diabetes, celiac disease, Multiple Sclerosis, Lupus, arthritis, and more, as previously discussed. These diseases are said to develop through first a genetic disposition, then through environmental triggers, such as infections and/or gut dysbiosis.

Many factors play a role in the development of autoimmunity. Tests can be done in the early stages of disease by testing an individual for autoantibodies (which are produced by the immune system and are directed against an individual's own proteins). Early symptoms of these diseases can be difficult to assess, so testing is important because progress in these diseases can be debilitating. Many of these diseases are documented to have major changes in the microbiome early on in development, so links to microbiome health and diversity are under investigation.

Dysbiosis of the gut microbiome can mean there are not enough good bacteria, or too many bad ones. In order to attain a balance, a regimen of eating higher fiber foods (prebiotics) and a good diversity of microbes (probiotics) will help bring the gut into balance. A balanced diet will also promote good cellular chemical cascades, creating the proper chemical balance in the gut to support a hormonal balance and therefore an enhanced gut-brain connection for improved mental health and just plain happiness.[56]

Diabetes

Considered an autoimmune disease, Diabetes was relatively uncommon and deadly, a hundred years ago. When the body stops producing insulin, sugar in the blood accumulates and concentrates the blood. Thus, an individual is unable to access glucose from their blood to provide energy for their body cells and systems. Not only does the blood thicken and sweeten from the sugar, the blood becomes so heavy and the molecules become so large that they are unable to pass through the blood capillaries. Eventually, cells at the extremities become starved and will die without blood treatments. The patient eventually will lose their extremities first (such as fingers, toes, ears, and nose) and without insulin, can die.

After the death of a friend in the summer of 1921, Frederick Banting and his colleague, Charles Best, successfully isolated insulin, using a professor's empty laboratory at the University of Toronto. With the development of insulin, diabetics needed to no longer suffer from this disease. Patients were then able to administer insulin through injections.

Sometimes, in the beginning of the diabetic stages, the disease can often be controlled through diet, because the pancreas is still functioning, to some level. Specific drugs and other treatments can also stimulate the pancreas to continue functioning for longer than it did in the past. However, the disease is on a disastrous rise, especially with younger and younger victims. At the same time, obesity is also on the rise. Our dependency on sugar and carbohydrates as a primary source of energy in our food system is something that is getting more and more attention nowadays.

Type 1 Diabetes

There are several types of Diabetes, not just one. Type 1 is the form whereby the patient's pancreas ceases to function and then dies, and was originally called juvenile Diabetes. This version is mostly seen in children and young adults, especially in children who are born with or soon develop a poorly functioning pancreas. The body attacks the pancreas for some reason, and it can take a short while or a long while to completely discontinue producing insulin for the body.

In the beginning of the pancreas's demise, the blood sugar level can often be treated with a monitored or lower-carbohydrate diet, sometimes replacing sugar with fat (called a ketogenic diet), thus keeping blood sugar levels more constant. Human bodies were meant to use more fat to burn as fuel, in our evolution, and much less sugar than we consume in our modern world.

Developing a flexible metabolism in light of the pancreas's demise is prudent. Consuming higher amounts of vegetables gives us plenty of carbohydrates to function at an optimum level. We need not consume processed food of any kind. In fact, processed foods are the major culprits of this disease. Lowering carbohydrates to deter full-blown Diabetes can often be a successful short-term and sometimes longer-term alternative to insulin, especially when progressing to the injection level.

Type 2 Diabetes

Type 2 Diabetes was long considered "adult-onset Diabetes" because those who developed this version created insulin resistance over longer periods of time. Usually, this stems from eating a high-calorie, high-sugar diet, which results in a developed insulin resistance. Then, ultimately, the need for outside insulin is induced. This type is no longer called "adult-onset Diabetes" because it is becoming commonplace with younger and younger patients. In fact, the youngest obese child in the world—a three-year-old in Texas, USA—was diagnosed with Type 2 Diabetes.

Some scientists agree that nearly 80% of the population in the USA and Canada is in various stages of insulin resistance or Diabetes, due to the high and growing sugar levels in the western diet.[57]

Type 3 Diabetes

Some recent research studies have proposed that Alzheimer's disease should also be classified as a type of Diabetes, called Type 3 Diabetes. "Type 3" is a term that has been proposed to describe the hypothesis that Alzheimer's disease, which is a major cause of dementia, is triggered by insulin resistance and an insulin-like growth factor dysfunction that occurs specifically in the brain. This dysfunction is similar to what happens in other parts of the body in people who have Types 1 and 2 Diabetes. This condition also has been used by some to describe people who have Type 2 Diabetes and are also diagnosed with Alzheimer's disease and dementia.[58] However, the classification of Type 3 Diabetes is controversial, and most doctors aren't ready to use it until more research is done, although it has been gaining momentum in the literature and certainly in the popular press.

Scientists have noticed the significant role diet plays in the development of plaque in a brain associated with Alzheimer's disease. Not only do we store fat on our bodies with high sugar ingestion, and not only do we develop insulin resistance so our pancreas needs to supply more and more insulin to allow the body to absorb the blood sugar, but this process lays down plaque in the brain as well. This correlation has been shown in rats. Human subject research is in its beginning stages. Finding this new breakthrough can seriously change how we look at prevention and cure of brain diseases of all sorts. Lowering our sugar intake as a cultural shift is looking more and more essential as a move towards physical and mental health generally speaking.

"Sugar" is a generic term and really boils down to mean blood sugar or sugar levels in your bloodstream. To be clear, one can avoid eating simple table sugar and still get Diabetes from eating high-sugar foods (such as baked goods and processed foods of all kinds) and having a general high-grain consumption. Sugar is largely found in fruits, root vegetables, and grains. It is also found on food product labels—by a myriad of other names.

Consumers must read labels when making choices of all, but especially processed foods, and go into food stores "armed" with a list of possibilities to look for and avoid.[59] Some examples include but are not limited to these different names for sugar: Agave nectar, Barbados sugar, barley malt, barley malt syrup, beet sugar, brown sugar, buttered syrup, cane juice, cane juice crystals, cane sugar, caramel, carob syrup, castor sugar, coconut palm sugar, coconut sugar, confectioner's sugar, corn sweetener, corn syrup, corn syrup solids, date sugar, dehydrated cane juice, demerara sugar, dextrin, dextrose, evaporated cane juice, free-flowing brown sugars, fructose, fruit juice, fruit juice concentrate, glucose, glucose solids, golden sugar, golden syrup, grape sugar, HFCS (High-Fructose Corn Syrup), honey, icing sugar, invert sugar, malt syrup, maltodextrin, maltol, maltose, mannose, maple syrup, molasses, muscovado, palm sugar, powdered sugar, raw sugar, refiner's syrup, rice syrup, saccharose, sorghum syrup, sucrose, sugar (granulated), sweet sorghum, syrup, treacle, turbinado sugar, and yellow sugar.

Other autoimmune diseases are similar to these three types of Diabetes in that diet or chemicals can often be the triggers that push us into dysbiosis and that dysfunction that begins in the gut. Such diseases include arthritis, celiac, Crohn's, Hashimoto's, Lupus, Multiple Sclerosis, and more.

Arthritis

Individuals with a family history of arthritis (the swelling and tenderness of one or more of your joints) or who have some early symptoms of it may also benefit greatly from a gluten-free and dairy-free diet, because both food groups are highly inflammatory and should be reduced or eliminated to inhibit the progress of the disease before joints are seriously compromised.

Collagen is also good for reducing inflammation of joints through healing a leaky gut. One of the best ways to approach healing a leaky gut is through consuming homemade bone broth, approximately 2-3 cups (500-750 mL) per day. This steady flow of collagen through the intestines brings material to the microbiome, which produces a mucosal lining of the GI tract to protect the actual cells of the intestinal wall. Because the construction of the gut wall is only one cell thick and goes directly into the bloodstream, not much protection is available if the mucus is not a healthy thickness. This can often be the first and best step to begin the gut-healing process and reduce inflammation throughout the entire body.

Celiac Disease[33] (as aforementioned)

Increasingly common in North America, celiac disease is considered to be "an allergy to gluten." As described previously, gluten is one of the worst culprits in creating Leaky Gut Syndrome and causing inflammation. Gluten should be reduced in the diet or avoided altogether.

Many (if not most of us) have gluten sensitivities from eating a long-term diet high in wheat flour and products thereof. Some people describe having gluten sensitivities, but this is not the same thing as celiac disease, because even those of us without celiac disease may damage the cells of our intestinal lining when eating gluten.[60]

Celiac disease (full-blown and lesser forms) is becoming so common that in 2019, it was found to be the root cause of a least fifty different diseases, including cancer, lymphoma, osteoporosis, kidney disease, and IBS, as well as other autoimmune diseases such as colitis, rheumatoid arthritis, and anemia. It is also a cause of psychiatric and neurological diseases such as anxiety, depression, schizophrenia, dementia, migraines, epilepsy, and Autism.[61]

Crohn's, Hashimoto's, Lupus, Multiple Sclerosis, and More[35,38,40,43] (as aforementioned)

Many autoimmune disease studies have shown that such diseases can possibly be prevented using probiotics, *including Type 1 Diabetes!* Researchers at the California Institute of Technology have estimated the sevenfold to eightfold increases in rates of autoimmune disorders is directly related to the lack of beneficial microbes in our gut.[62] Ongoing research will give us more information on this front, but data thus far shows that it does not hurt and in some cases helps considerably.[63]

Some evidence shows that certain microbes or combinations of gut flora (in their excrement) are responsible for creating the particular chemicals needed to protect against certain deficiencies which can create the symptoms of particular diseases. This area of research (particular bacteria for particular disease prevention) is very active at the current time and forecasts are that this could be a huge new area of healthcare in the future.

The food-mood connection is described in great detail in this chapter. Our balance of gut microbes, proper prebiotic/probiotic intake, and the prevention or recovery from LGS are keys to gut health as well as brain health. Once the gut lining is damaged, small food particles enter the bloodstream, creating the potential for inflammation anywhere in the body. Our mood and mental health problems (ADD/ADHD, anxiety, depression, headaches, and more) occur when we have inflammation in the brain. This is the gut-brain-microbiome connection.

Chapter 5—Key Highlights:

1. The human gut microbiome (known as our "second brain") begins at the birth inoculation and consists of a community of one-celled organisms.

2. Our gut microbiome protects our GI tract which is a giant filter between our intake (food and drink) and our blood system. Our gut microbiota provides seven functions (outlined in the diagram near the beginning of the chapter). This filter is only one cell thick, so the health of it collectively deserves our attention and intention to nourish it, to protect our overall health and maintain a closely knit and sealed gut.

3. LGS occurs when our gut lining tears and food particles enter our bloodstream, causing inflammation to our GI tract. Inflammation is known to be the underlying cause of a multitude of diseases and can spread through the bloodstream to wherever we have some type of weakness.

4. Natural antibiotics are compounds produced by bacteria and fungi, which are capable of killing or inhibiting competing microbial species. Over-prescribed

antibiotics are now in our water systems in a large supply. They are in our drinking water, our rivers, and our oceans. They kill important microbes on ALL BIOMES now, and are endangering the extinction of all species.

5. Antibiotics kill microbial life indiscriminately. When good bacteria are depleted, they must be replenished with probiotics, in order for a person to return to health.

6. Probiotics are live organisms that consist of particular bacterial strains and yield health benefits on their hosts.

7. Prebiotics (varieties of fiber) are essential foods for the microbes (probiotics) who live on us and in us. Prebiotics are not digestible by humans. We actually need the help of probiotics to digest fiber, so we can maintain the balance needed (in our microbiome) for good health.

8. Certain varieties of microbes contribute to certain functions of our metabolism and food absorption. Health benefits of probiotics include improving mineral absorption, modulating the immune system, modulating satiety, improving bowel habits (reducing occasional constipation and diarrhea), promoting metabolic health, improving symptoms of IBS, reducing risks of allergies of all sorts, and supporting energy balance and glucose metabolism.

9. Our microbes must be fed properly, in order to maintain balance in the population and avoid dysbiosis. Dysbiosis is an imbalance in the bacteria in our gut microbiome and can lead to a leaky gut and inflammation.

10. Without microbiome health and balance, we are susceptible to a variety of diseases.

11. As the junctions between cells weaken, and the molecules of food and waste permeate the blood, a leaky gut occurs.

12. Autoimmunity begins in the unbalanced and leaky gut.

13. Our gut is only one cell thick and consists of the entire digestive tract—mouth, throat, esophagus, stomach, upper or small intestine/bowel, pancreas, liver, lower or large intestine/bowel, and anus.

14. Gluten tears our gut lining every time we ingest it. The microbiome community assists the immune system in healing the gut lining. Our bodies can repair the tears, but only for so long. When we can no longer repair the damage, inflammation occurs, which can cause a multitude of diseases.

15. Three specific factors must all be present for the actual disease to result: genetic susceptibility, exposure to inflammatory antigens (invading microbes or pathogens), and a damaged gut lining.

16. Collagen and cartilage (found in tendons, joints, and gristle of animal products) are great for helping heal inflammation and a leaky gut. Consuming 2-3 cups of bone broth on a daily basis brings material to the microbiome, which produces a mucosal lining of the GI tract to protect the actual cells of the intestinal wall.

17. Our microbiome is an important foundation for our immunity, mood/mental health, and our weight management.

18. We can improve our health if we follow the guidelines set out by Canada and Brazil.

19. Sugars are dangerous when consumed in high volumes and are known by a plethora of names, so it is important for consumers to read food labels and buy accordingly!

Chapter 6: The Brain and Consciousness

Until recent times, it was thought that the brain resided in a completely sterile environment and was separated from the body through membranes. It was long assumed that we were born with a set number of neurons in our brains and we stopped growing them early in life. Throughout my lifetime, it was widely accepted that we had only one way to go with our brains, and that was downhill—via a brain cell loss! We were not aware of the possibility of growing neurons and new neural pathways. It was only through major recoveries of people with severe brain and spinal cord damage that we witnessed regrowth and improved function.

Christopher Reeve, the actor who played the star in the *Superman* movies, was an accomplished equestrian and was thrown dramatically from his horse. The result was a debilitating break of his spine. Because he was wealthy and determined to recover, he made great progress through intense physical therapy and was able to recreate neural pathways to be able to regain function, although limited, in his arms and legs.[64] At that point, scientists and disabled people all over the world were greatly encouraged with his progress and much hope for spinal injury rehabilitation was ignited. People who have had severe brain injuries and people who have had pieces of their brain removed (due to disease) have been known to regain function, in many cases. Amazingly, about 100 children a year have half of their brain removed, particularly when they are afflicted with Rasmussen's encephalitis (a rare inflammatory neurological disease), where severe seizures prompt the procedure to be attempted as a last resort.[65]

Many people attend special schools if they have learning disabilities such as dyslexia or to heal a traumatic brain injury (TBI). Based on Barbara Arrowsmith-Young's experiences in changing her own brain (documented in *The Woman Who Changed Her Brain*[66]), such schools use hand-eye practice and a variety of exercises to target a specific brain territory. Barbara used those exercises to heal her learning difficulties through self-commitment and dedicated practice over several years. Her results inspired books and schools in both Canada and Australia. (The Eaton Arrowsmith School is located in Vancouver, B.C., for example.)

Neuroplasticity (brain plasticity) research has entirely changed the way we look at the brain. We now see that it grows and changes throughout our lifetime. It is not static; it is neuroplastic!

The Brain: Its Structure and Function

The human brain is a highly evolved and complex organ. Modern man considers it to be the most sophisticated brain on Earth. In fact, for most of human history, we have thought that we are superior to all other life on Earth. Considering the success of the human race and our accomplishments, this high intelligence and sophistication can be debated (depending on how one assesses intelligence). Certainly, we are the most complicated. Fortunately, we have evolved enough now to ascertain just how much trouble we have created for ourselves and the rest of life on our planet.

Despite our evolution and great developments over the million-plus years of history of our species, according to cognitive neuroscientists, we are *conscious* of only 10-12% of our brain's activity, so most of our decisions, actions, emotions, and behaviors depends on the 88% of brain activity that goes beyond our conscious awareness. We refer to this as our subconscious or unconscious part of our brain or mind.[67] (Later in the chapter, we will go into detail and discuss these parts of the mind.)

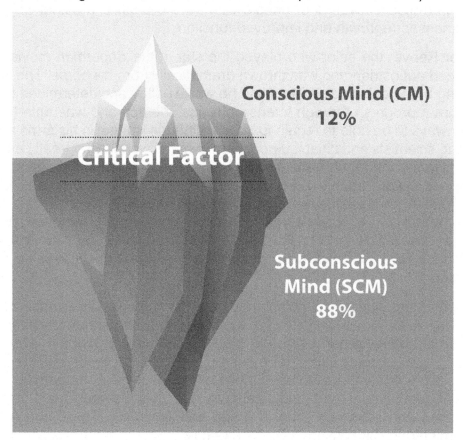

Considering humans are such deep-thinking and creative organisms, it is fascinating to consider that this much of our brains or minds operate at the subconscious or unconscious level! As a result, almost ALL human functions occur beneath our conscious awareness. We don't have to think about breathing, beating our hearts, digesting our food, or replacing skin cells. We are not aware of our hair and fingernails growing or the complexity of our endocrine system. If we were aware of it all, we couldn't function at all—it would be much too much for us to think about!

We are also mostly *not* aware of our communication with others. Many of us believe that we communicate only with our words. For example, we come up with ideas, then we speak them and/or write about them, but the truth is that this is a small part of the total of our communication. We now know that we communicate in non-verbal ways, too.

We are also often raised without a complete vocabulary to identify or describe how we feel, to others—or to ourselves. Most of this happens at our subconscious level, causing us to be aware only when the emotion and then a physical feeling has taken a hold in our bodies. We then become consciously aware of what is happening. For example, our body is shaking, we feel terror, or get a rush of adrenaline (such as when someone cuts us off in traffic). However, most of us don't realize that our experience of emotion arises due to our *perception* of an experience and is subject to our *interpretation of the experience*, when compared to events in our past.

What does this mean?

Most of our actions and reactions to life happen at the subconscious level. For example, Cal Banyan (a speaker, an author, a certified professional hypnosis instructor, and the founder of both the Banyan Hypnosis Centre and the 5-Path Method of hypnosis[68]) uses the following "equation" to explain how we humans *create our own reality* based upon the meaning we give to events in our world. In this scenario, the left side of the vertical line occurs in our brain or mind and the right side is a physical reaction to it in our body.

$$X \rightarrow M \rightarrow E \rightarrow | \rightarrow F \rightarrow B \rightarrow X$$

Brain | Body

In this model,

X $\rightarrow$ represents an *event*. In actuality, an event is inherently neutral, but we humans assign the event a meaning. The meaning will be positive or negative, based on our previous experience (feels "good" or "bad"). It is also grounded in our childhood worldview.

M $\rightarrow$ is the *meaning* we assign an event. We assess it based on memories of emotions that we experienced early in life. Some suggest that this is from our first three years. The emotional reaction is sorted into our SCM as either a positive or negative.

Our assessments are based on very simple assertions such as "pain versus pleasure" or "known versus unknown," which are then stored in our memory around a certain "event."

If you think about any event, there can be several people in attendance, but each person will have his or her own experience of the event, in accordance to their expectations based on past experiences. Each of those individuals will have their own ideas and connections to past experiences—all different, even if they were all at the same event, and even if they are from the same family and were present at the same series of events!

E → is the *emotion* that is triggered in the brain from that assessment. The decision is to decide whether or not it is positively or negatively charged, and a resulting emotion will be decided. This process happens in nanoseconds, at the subconscious level. Emotions of fear, anger, guilt, sadness, joy, elation, desire, and nostalgia all begin in the brain, which then gets transmitted to the body. This is then where we become aware of it, because we feel it in our physical body.

F → is the physical *feeling* that the mental emotion triggers in the body. It can be transmitted by electrical currents, through the nerves/nervous system, or by the chemistry of the hormonal/endocrine system. Either way, it happens in less than an instant. This can be for example, a rush of adrenaline, a shiver, pounding heart, or a craving of some sort.

B → represents the *behavior* induced by the feeling in the body. Reactions might include eating to satisfy a craving, crying for a sadness, avoidance due to a fear, lying due to guilt, etc. Behaviors become ingrained as habits that we do automatically. Because we are distracted by the behavior, we get a short-term reward, but this does nothing to change the chain of events. This is fine, if this habit works for us—and many do, for some time. However, as time goes on, there can come a point where this automatic pilot behavior no longer works for us, and it can be difficult to be aware of it when it is happening or change the habit if we want to. This is why changing habits through sheer willpower can be incredibly difficult.

To summarize, we attach meaning to an event that produces an emotional interpretation based purely on past experiences. All of this is processed in the Subconscious Mind (SCM) to create an emotional reaction.

The emotion can then be transferred from the brain to the body, which will produce a physical feeling. These physical feelings are created either electrically, through the Vagus nerve response, or hormonally (endocrinologically), through chemical reactions dispersed throughout the bloodstream.

Our SCM is our emotional mind, which controls our bodily functions and behaviors, most of which we are totally unaware. As such, we can consciously observe our behaviors or habits, which are results of our early programming, to become aware of our belief structure.

Our programming is the result of repetitive events, beliefs, and habits that surround us from our family of origin and other socializations in our Near Environment. This saves us a lot of time and energy, because we do a lot of things in our lives without even thinking about them—they happen automatically.

However, as a result of this, when bad habits develop, they can be very difficult to change because they must be changed at the subconscious level.

Evolution has built several automatic systems in our brains. These allow a quick response to dangers in our environment and we never have to actually *think* about the reaction.

The limbic system is one such system, and it is a very important system that allows us to stay safe (alive) in the face of danger. The limbic system forms what is commonly called our *fight, flight, or freeze response.* It combines higher mental functions and primitive emotions into one system. It puts our bodies on high alert when we are in danger and has been integral to allowing our species to survive enough to grow and evolve to the technologically sophisticated species we are today. Despite our advances in these technologically specialized fields, we are still essentially the animals from which we evolved, so even though we rarely have instances where we need to run from a tiger in the bushes, we still react hormonally from the chemistry in this system on a daily basis.

The limbic system is often referred to as AHH, due to its components. The major parts of the human brain limbic system are the amygdala, the hippocampus, and the hypothalamus. An easy way to remember these parts is through the acronym AAH.

AHH = Limbic System Structures

A: Amygdala

The amygdala is the emotion center of the brain. This little almond-shaped mass of nuclei is involved in emotional responses, hormonal secretions, and memory. The amygdala is responsible for fear conditioning, which is the associative learning process by which we learn to fear something. When you feel a jolt at a large noise, for example, your amygdala releases a drop of adrenaline.

We easily remember events when strong emotions, trauma, or extreme joy are involved—even when they occur at a very young age. This is part of how the amygdala is tied to our memory.

When our body is highly charged with any kind of excitement, fear, or high levels of stress, cortisol is released into the bloodstream. Because our body is on high alert, and we are full of adrenaline and cortisol, our brains can only maintain this imbalance for short bursts of time. This part of the system was never meant to be in service for long periods of time because our brains cannot be fully engaged when we are on high alert.

H: Hippocampus

This part of the limbic system is a tiny "nub" in the brain that acts as a memory indexer, sending memories out to the appropriate part of the cerebral hemisphere for long-term storage and retrieving them when necessary. While the hippocampus plays an essential role in the formation of new memories about past experiences, the thalamus and hypothalamus are associated with changes in emotional reactivity.

H: Hypothalamus

This piece of the system is about the size of a pearl and directs a multitude of important functions. It wakes you up in the morning and gets your adrenaline flowing. It directs unconscious functions such as body temperature, hunger, and homeostasis. The hypothalamus is also an important emotional center, controlling the molecules that make you feel exhilarated, angry, or unhappy.

The hypothalamic-pituitary-adrenal axis stimulates adrenal glands during times of stress to create cortisol, the body's key stress response hormone. Higher levels of cortisol correlate to a variety of issues, including depression and Alzheimer's disease.[69] An elevated cortisol level also has damaging effects on the gut flora, changing the mix of gut bacteria. Chronic high cortisol levels also increase permeability of the gut lining, leading to inflammation.

Therefore, high cortisol levels increase inflammation, increase gut lining permeability, increase Leaky Gut Syndrome—and all of this leads to more susceptibility to mood disorders.

The good news is that this can all be supported or even reversed by ingesting probiotics—in particular, *Bifidobacterium infantis*. This particular bacterium shows that microbial gut bugs, rather than just our brain alone, can contribute to and even control our response to stress. This particular microbe, *Bifidobacterium infantis,* is found in many common fermented foods, such as some yogurt, olives, sauerkraut, salami, and cheeses. In recent times, it has also been added to some infant formulas. Read your labels for particular strains.

As you can see, these tiny brain participants play a huge role in our emotional life, in good ways and bad ways. Ultimately, it is our perception of the event, the resulting emotions in our brains, and the physical feelings which occur that determine our reactions or behavior in response to an event. Fortunately, perceptions can be altered to reframe things before they develop into issues that can deter our success.

Fight, Flight, or Freeze Response

The fight, flight, or freeze response directs our body to put almost everything except essential services on hold while there is any perceived danger. Immediately, when we sense danger, such as a "tiger in the grass," our body redirects the blood supply away from our internal organs (such as our digestive tract) to the areas in our body that are necessary to make quick decisions and react with speed and strength. This means blood goes to our brains for thinking and to our limbs FOR RUNNING! This enables us to get out of there and climb a tree, if that's what we need to do. There are many documented examples of people moving incredibly large, fallen objects in a feat of super-human strength, such as when a family member is stuck under a car, for example. This ability is actually called "hysterical strength" and has been documented many times in history.[70]

When we react to such a situation, our body reacts immediately and releases adrenaline. Adrenaline keeps our brain on high alert so we can think clearly while running to find safety as soon as possible. Our heart and blood pumps very fast, our ability to run fast and long is enhanced, and our muscles become stronger.

Unconscious Incompetence → Conscious Competence

As society has become more technological and complicated, and the pace has increased, stress from normal day-to-day life has increased exponentially. We experience a huge number of stimuli from all around us, even for things that we now consider commonplace, such as driving our car on a normal commute from the suburbs to the downtown of a city. Consider all the steps and training that have to be in place to operate a motor vehicle on a freeway, merge in and out of traffic, find new locations, operate accessories, possibly even eat, and change the radio station. As we learn new skills in our modern-day life, they become commonplace and we do them almost automatically. They do, however, take their toll on our base stress level. The good thing about learning a new skill is that practice increases our competence in any task, and the stress of learning a new skill diminishes over the course of the growing competency.

When learning a complex grouping of behaviors, the process of moving from unconscious incompetence to unconscious competence involves four stages.

Let's look at each stage in detail, using the example of learning to drive a car that has a manual transmission.

1. At the stage of unconscious incompetence or "not knowing what we don't know," we cannot even see the problem, let alone have a clue about the solution. Here, we ignorant and are like "a fish in water," so to speak.

2. At the stage of conscious incompetence, we realize we actually don't know something. We then set out to learn it. We become the "fish out of water." Life is hard and there is too much stimuli. We need to find that sweet spot where you let the clutch out just right, before you push on the gas pedal.

3. At the stage of conscious competence, we begin to learn a new skill, but cannot do it very well right away. We stumble, we fall, and it takes a lot of mental capacity to operate. We know we don't know something but we want to know it, so we practice, then we practice more. We go from bad to not so bad. We succeed and we fail. We stall and bunny-hop, getting into first gear, but lurch, going into second gear.

4. Finally, at the stage of unconscious competence, we get it! We can do it AND the task becomes second nature. We can shift smoothly through all the gears without thinking too much.

Eventually, we can drive and perform other functions and activities at the same time. We can walk and chew gum! The task or skill is easy, smooth, and stress-free. It almost seems like it is automatic. At this stage, we have developed a habit through repetition. It is both mental and physical, and it went from the conscious mind to the subconscious.

The diagram shows the progression from one stage to the next.

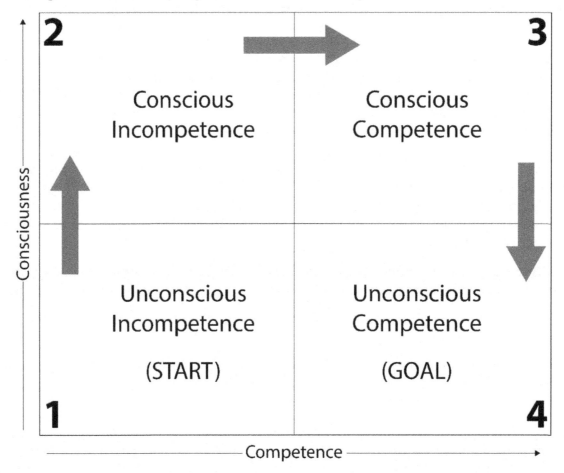

Once unconscious competence is achieved, it means we have developed a habit and we can do it without being conscious of what needs to happen every second. The best example of this is learning to drive a stick shift, as described, which takes more coordination that driving a car that has an automatic transmission.

Eventually, with practice, we develop an unconscious competence with all of our skills. This is nature's way of making our lives more efficient. However, even knowing we can competently perform many tasks concurrently (including "running the mental tapes" about how we think and feel about certain things), the trouble is that the learned skills, habits of body, and habits of thought operate at a subconscious level in the background and never stop. Because we continue to pile more and more on top of everything we learn, as we grow, it sometimes gets to be too much—especially if we don't let things go, at lower levels of priority. The number of stimuli that we consciously ignore but which still stress us at a subconscious level is astounding. Our brains are constantly looking for ways to decrease amounts of and levels of stress, and ultimately to file it into an unconscious state.

For an easy example of this, think of those who live by railroads, hospitals, or near airports. The first few weeks of living so close to such loud noises, especially when they are not used to it, people have difficulty sleeping, concentrating, and feeling calm. They are awakened constantly by signals, sirens, or other noises in the night and often have trouble getting back to sleep. The great thing about our brain is that it learns to filter those annoyances and label them as just "background noise." Eventually, most people don't hear it or feel bothered by it at all. Our brains learn to treat it as insignificant background noise and filter it out to the point where we can become completely unaware of it.

How Stress Affects the Microbiome

Stress on our limbic system is necessary when we are living in the wild, in jungles or on savannas, along with wild animals. That kind of stress is "on" for an instant, and then it shuts "off," when the danger has passed. In modern times, we don't really need such alarms unless they are quite necessary, such as when an unwanted fire starts, perhaps during our sleep, or some other similar occurrence. It is not necessary or healthy to have that kind of intense reaction happening in our bodies on a constant and daily basis. Yet that is what has transpired in modern times: chronic (non-stop), long-term, amazingly high stress levels.

Chronic stress releases a nearly constant source of cortisol into the bloodstream. High levels of cortisol can wear down the brain's ability to function properly. Stress kills brain cells and even reduces the size of the brain. In particular, chronic stress has a shrinking effect on the prefrontal cortex, which is the area of the brain responsible for memory and learning. Chronic stress then inhibits our abilities to focus and learn. Stress also plays havoc with the health and diversity of the microbiome population. Stress actually has a very strong detrimental effect on our gut environment as well as the brain because they are in constant connection and communication.

Stress, anxiety, and the cortisol released affects the health of our microbiome. So, it is not just what we eat but how we feel (and the resulting chemistry released into our bodies) that affects the microbiome. This is another example of the gut-brain connection. Therefore, the Internal Environment (created by the type and treatment of food we eat), plus the reaction to the external environment (emotional reactions, fears, and stressors) affect our gut and its inhabitants.

Other factors can also be involved.

Neural transmitters throughout our bodies communicate between the gut and the brain. As previously mentioned, the Vagus nerve is the chief communicator between the gut and brain. There is a constant, two-way communication transmission between the brain and the lower gut (mostly our large intestines) at all times. Neural transmitters, a variety of hormones, and other stimulants communicate between the gut and brain. The "butterflies in your stomach" feeling of excitement or the "don't go ahead with that" reaction are real, emotional, and intuitive reactions to subliminal or subconscious cues around you.[71]

Our subconscious mind is greatly affected by our microbiome in our memory, our emotional reactions, and our resulting behaviours. When things become habits, we don't even have to think about them. In fact, we are not even consciously aware of our habits or our paradigms—or the thought patterns that create them.

Not only do the neural pathways between gut and brain notify each other and our conscious mind, but chemicals from our endocrine system are also distributed through our blood supply to communicate with other parts of our body to cue our thoughts, feelings, and in particular, our behaviors. These behaviors can be affected through working on our microbiome health and balance as well as working through our subconscious or emotional mind. The microbiome comprises a huge grouping of microbes, which are a part of our subconscious mind, and form feelings, cravings, and intuitions that dramatically affect our habits and behaviours at the subconscious level.

Our Five Brainwaves

Humans experience and operate in a variety of brainwaves. The five most common are gamma, beta, alpha, theta, and delta. Each brainwave has a distinct purpose and helps us think, feel, behave, move, and process in different ways and at different levels of awareness. Although brainwaves change channels automatically, our own ability to modulate between them determines our ability to cope with pressure, rational and irrational thoughts, task management, and more.[72] That is why it is important to be aware of the different states available to us, and recognize our ability to change our state of mind, if needed. (More information about these "different states" will soon follow.)

It is important for us all to develop some kind of a daily "practice," to become resilient in our use of these "different states" in our personal growth and development. If our physiology, diet, or environment causes an overproduction or an underproduction of a certain brainwave, it can alter the balance of our bodies and induce many negative effects (such as insomnia, anger, stress, anxiety, or learning difficulties). That is why it is so important to optimize our brains for a better wave balance, rather than aim to increase or decrease a particular one.

Brainwave Frequency and the Different States Associated with Each

In normal, day-to-day life, our brainwaves are portioned or divided into ranges of frequencies or speeds of the wave, technically called "hertz" (Hz). Hertz is the frequency of the peak of the waves (close together versus farther apart).

In order of lowest to highest frequency, the five brainwaves are delta, theta, alpha, beta, and gamma brainwaves. Although we'll go into detail for each one, you can refer to the diagram of the five brainwave patterns and the descriptions included in it, for a better understanding of the different brainwaves and where/when they might appear.

The wave frequency pictorials will provide help you in visualizing the difference between the states (for example, how experiencing a different brainwave might feel, or what that brainwave is good at, or what might likely be happening while one experiences this particular state).

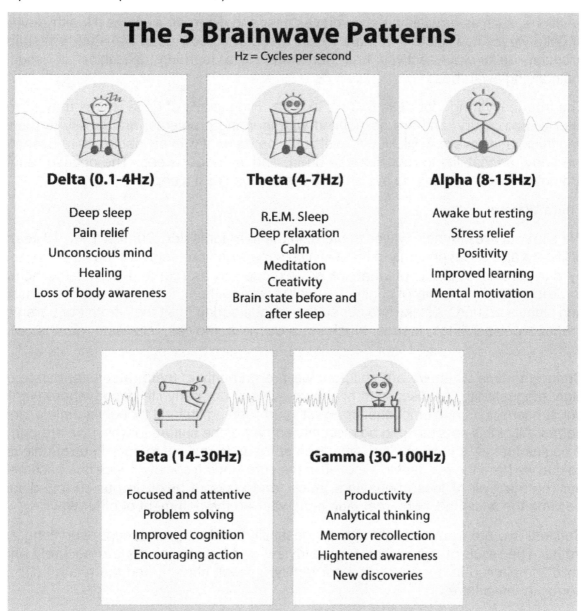

The 5 Brainwave Patterns

Hz = Cycles per second

Delta (0.1-4Hz)

Deep sleep
Pain relief
Unconscious mind
Healing
Loss of body awareness

Theta (4-7Hz)

R.E.M. Sleep
Deep relaxation
Calm
Meditation
Creativity
Brain state before and after sleep

Alpha (8-15Hz)

Awake but resting
Stress relief
Positivity
Improved learning
Mental motivation

Beta (14-30Hz)

Focused and attentive
Problem solving
Improved cognition
Encouraging action

Gamma (30-100Hz)

Productivity
Analytical thinking
Memory recollection
Hightened awareness
New discoveries

Delta Waves

Delta waves are often called "deep sleep brainwaves," associated with deep levels of relaxation as well as restorative sleep. (Simply think of "delta" for "deep.") They are the slowest recorded brainwaves in humans. Higher amounts of these are more commonly found in young children, who go in and out of sleep very easily. When we age, lower delta waves are produced, and we seem to achieve those delta deep states for shorter times.

Research tells us that delta waves are attributed to many of our unconscious bodily functions, such as regulating the cardiovascular and digestive systems. Healthy levels of delta waves contribute to a more restful sleep and allow us to wake up refreshed. Irregular delta wave activity has been linked to learning difficulties or issues maintaining awareness.

The frequency range for delta is 0 Hz to 4 Hz. High levels of delta waves may occur after a brain injury, and are associated with learning problems, an inability to focus and think, and severe ADHD. Low levels may be present with an inability to rejuvenate the body, an inability to revitalize the brain, and with poor sleep. The optimal range promotes a healthy immune system and restorative REM sleep.

Theta Waves

We start our lives in theta waves in utero, in the third trimester. Our first 10 to 12 years of life are also spent primarily in theta, which serves and protects us in being socialized by our parents. We accept what we are exposed to as real and true in the home environment of our family of origin. Everything we see, hear, feel, and learn from those and what is around us sinks into our subconscious during this time—from our parents, grandparents, siblings, friends, teachers, preachers, movies, television, games, and more.

During the time when we are children, we are primarily in theta, a constant state of high suggestibility. As discussed previously, this is our early life period where we fill our subconscious and emotional brain with surrounding cultural thoughts, beliefs, and norms. All of this sets us up to be a socialized part of the culture in which we are born. It begins first as a family culture and then spreads to our entire social surroundings, so that we have the mindset to succeed in the surrounding society. Since this becomes our "normal," all of these behaviors, roles, and ways of being in our surroundings become the accepted, right, real, and best way—to the detriment of other ways.

Because we are in a state of "high suggestibility" in theta, we accept everything as truths. The result of this is that our worldview and belief systems are securely and solidly implanted in our psyche by our family, school, church, and the related social norms in the culture.

Nowadays, our constant exposure to media and social media precipitates a substantial role in this early development as well.

Theta waves are known as the "suggestible waves" because of their prevalence when one is in a trance, a meditative state, or a hypnotic state. In such a state, the brain's theta waves are optimal, and an individual is more susceptible to hypnosis and associated therapy. The reasoning for this is that theta waves are commonly found while daydreaming or when asleep, thus exhibiting a more relaxed, open mind-state.

Theta waves are also linked to experiencing and feeling deep and raw emotions. The problem is that too much theta activity may make people prone to bouts of depression. Theta, however, has benefits of helping improve creativity, wholeness, intuition, and feeling more "natural." Like delta waves, theta waves are also involved in restorative sleep. As long as theta waves aren't produced in excess during our waking hours, it is a very helpful brainwave range.

The frequency range for theta brainwaves is 4 Hz to 8 Hz. Higher levels of theta waves occur in ADHD or hyperactivity, depressive states, impulsive activity, and inattentiveness. Lower levels are common during anxiety, poor emotional awareness, and higher stress levels. The optimal range supports maximum creativity, deep emotional connection with oneself and others, greater intuition, and deep relaxation.

Alpha Waves

Alpha waves are the "frequency bridge" between our conscious thinking (beta) and subconscious (theta) mind. They are known to help calm you down and promote feelings of deep relaxation and contentment. As we grow and develop, beta waves play an active role in network coordination and communication and do not usually occur until three years of age in humans.

In a state of stress, a phenomenon called "alpha blocking" can occur, which involves excessive beta activity and little alpha activity. In that scenario, the beta waves restrict the production of alpha because our body is reacting positively to the increased beta activity—usually in a state of heightened cognitive arousal, such as when heightened learning occurs.

The frequency range for alpha brainwaves is from 8 Hz to 12 Hz. With high levels of alpha, there can be too much daydreaming, an over-relaxed state, or an inability to focus. With low levels of alpha, OCD, anxiety symptoms, and higher stress levels occur. The optimal range is the ideal relaxation frequency.

Beta Waves

Beta waves are the high frequency brainwaves most commonly found in our normal waking state. They are channeled during conscious states, such as cognitive reasoning, calculation, reading, speaking, or thinking. Higher levels of beta waves are found to channel a stimulating, arousing effect, which explains how the brain will limit the number of alpha waves if heightened beta activity occurs. However, if you experience too much beta activity, this may lead to overwhelm, stress, and anxiety during strenuous periods of work or school.

Beta waves are increased by drinking common stimulants, such as caffeine. You can think of beta as the "get stuff done" state of mind. Beta states also include an increased willpower and decision-making ability.

The frequency range for beta brainwaves is 12 Hz to 40 Hz. High levels of beta are linked with anxiety, an inability to feel relaxed, high adrenaline levels, and high stress. Low levels of beta are common during depression, poor cognitive ability, and a lack of attention or focus. The optimal range will be consistent focus, strong memory recall, and a high problem-solving ability.

Gamma Waves

Gamma waves are a more recent discovery in the field of neuroscience. Thus, the understanding of how they function is evolving. To date, it's known that gamma waves are involved in processing more complex tasks, in addition to contributing to a healthy cognitive function. Gamma waves are important for learning, memory, and processing. They are used as a binding tool for our senses to process new information.

In people with mental disabilities, much lower levels of gamma activity are recorded. More recently, a strong link between meditation and gamma waves has been found—a link attributed to the heightened state of being or "completeness" experienced when in a meditative state.

The frequency range for gamma brainwaves is 40 Hz to 100 Hz. High levels of gamma are linked to anxiety and stress. Low levels are linked to depression, ADHD, and learning issues. The optimal range is good for information processing, cognition, learning, and the binding of senses (sight, smell, and hearing).

Since describing in detail the different types of brainwaves (in particular, alpha and theta), it makes sense to discuss the practices of meditation and hypnosis next.

Meditation and Hypnosis

Meditation has been practiced for thousands of years. Hypnosis has been documented for hundreds of years and is suspected to have been practiced since early Sumerian, Persian, Chinese Indian Greek Roman, and Egyptian times.[73]

According to the Yoga Synergy website, the true meaning of meditation is defined as follows:

Meditation is a loose term referring to any of a family of practices in which the practitioner trains their mind or self-induces a mode of consciousness in order to realize some benefits. Loosely, meditation refers to the state of mind when you are in yoga (in union of body, mind and spirit), and actually means yoga (union).[74]

In this instance, "union" is not necessarily the more physical practice of yoga that we are familiar with in the west. In meditation training, one receives and/or uses a single mantra (word or short phrase) that is received from the trained meditation teacher or "guru." The practice usually consists of repeating the mantra accompanied with a mindful slowing of the breath, until the mind and body calms. Many describe the experience as "emptying the mind." When the brainwaves calm, the body calms, resulting in lowered heartrate, blood pressure, and other physical indicators. Brainwaves begin to change, starting from conscious beta, slowing to alpha, and then to theta. Different styles of meditation exist, but the processes are relatively similar.

Meditation has been widely scientifically studied and has been proven to have many physical and psychological benefits.

The beginnings of meditation in the west came through Maharishi Mahesh Yogi, who developed a specific technique for the western world called Transcendental Meditation (TM). TM now has millions of practitioners around the world, including a university and several schools in many North American cities.[75]

During TM, the practitioner repeats a specific personal mantra. When combined with mindful awareness and the slowing of breath, this slows down other systems in the body—the heartbeat, blood pressure, and other brainwaves—and allows theta brainwaves to predominate. These simple slowings promote increased health through relaxation and stress reduction. The process is easy to learn, but it takes repetition (just as with any other skill) to enable a new student to become familiar and comfortable with the practice. Over the long term, meditation can promote health and wellness in many areas of life. Much research has been done over the last 40 years to determine the benefits of meditation.[76]

Hypnosis

Hypnosis is not sleep nor just relaxation. It's a state of mind where you are highly receptive to positive suggestions.

According to WebMD, hypnosis, also called hypnotherapy, *uses guided relaxation, intense concentration, and focused attention to achieve a heightened state of awareness that is sometimes called a trance. The person's attention is so focused while in this state that anything going on around the person is temporarily blocked out or ignored.*[77]

Hypnosis is a very natural state. You are always conscious and alert, just extremely relaxed in your body.

Hypnosis can help you change your habits, reduce the sensation of pain, increase motivation, help heal from past experiences, find lost items, eliminate fear, assist with spiritual growth, and aid you with many other everyday issues.

A fact unknown to many, hypnosis is a natural state that we pass through at least twice a day—when we fall asleep and when we awaken. We also go in and out of hypnosis when we do repetitive things, such as walking, running, skiing, driving, knitting, spinning, stirring, writing, listening to great music, reading a good book, and watching a good movie. In those instances, we become an observer and are slightly removed from the reality of what is going on.

Hypnosis is and has been a recognized medical application, by both the American and Canadian Medical Associations, since 1954. It is not new and it is not dangerous. It is commonly used in European hospitals for general pain (when patients are unable or unwilling to use anesthetics) or for childbirth. It is also commonly used for smoking cessation. In fact, during a recent visit to France, almost everyone I met had used hypnosis to quit smoking!

Some people think or believe that hypnosis is mind control, which is incorrect. That is a staged hypnotist performance, for entertainment only. Subjects in such a performance are chosen for their obvious suggestibility and are often removed from the stage when they are discovered to be no longer in hypnosis or pretend to be hypnotized. You are always in control when in hypnosis and you cannot be forced to do anything you would not normally do.

This is key for the uninitiated to know: the only kind of hypnosis, really, is self-hypnosis. Thus, a hypnotist is merely a skilled facilitator or guide. When doing therapeutic hypnosis, the client discusses in depth what their personal issues are. Hypnosis can then be specifically geared towards solving stubborn issues, all with the client's permission and intention. The client sets the stage and the hypnotherapist facilitates the process, in which the client transforms past experiences to develop deeper understanding through adult perspectives.

Self-hypnosis, like meditation, can be easily taught and is a very useful tool for personal growth and development—for either changing unwanted thoughts, feelings, or behaviors, or for enhancing and developing wanted ones. Therefore, it becomes an invaluable tool for personal development of all kinds, whether they be solving problems of unwanted habits, thoughts, or behaviors or developing wanted NEW thoughts, feelings, habits, or behaviors.

Hypnosis taps into the power of the subconscious mind, where our memories and emotions are stored. Experience has shown that when someone is in a trance, memories are accessible from the time in the womb and even from conception. Some people have even attested to accessing memories from previous lifetimes during hypnosis, although my clients and I have no such experiences thus far.

Many world religions include a belief in life after death as well as in this phenomenon of reincarnation, which seems to add to the mystery for some. Unfortunately, it also the reason that some people disbelieve in hypnosis altogether as a credible technique.

Hypnosis and meditation are similar in that we purposefully change our brainwaves to the point where we reach the alpha state or the deeper theta state. With meditation, it may take practicing individuals a lifetime to learn techniques well enough to consistently reach deep states quickly. Hypnosis, in contrast, is fast and easy.

With a guide, hypnosis is also extremely powerful. Because we can easily access deep and unconscious memories, the ability to resolve or remove past and erroneous perceptions and misunderstandings is quite different from meditating. That is the magic of hypnosis. Using certain techniques, such things can be "reframed" and essentially resolved. This allows for the release of unwanted emotions and thus the automatic, subconscious beliefs and their resulting feelings and behaviors. When we are not consciously aware of what subconscious thoughts and consequent emotional reactions our body is having, we can be running subconscious "programming" of thoughts, feelings, and behaviors, of which we are not even aware. This phenomenon can drastically affect our relationships and our long-term mental, physical, and emotional health. In that way, hypnosis and "subconscious work" can dramatically affect our lives by helping us to become aware of our beliefs. In doing that, we can then change our unwanted unconscious habits, which can be extremely difficult to do using willpower alone.

Brainwave Activity—The Different States and Our Feelings

The brain is a complex network of billions of cells called neurons that communicate with one another via electrochemical impulses. The chemicals are hormones that are produced by various organs in the body, the brain, and the microbiome. The brain and the gut are in constant contact, back and forth with each other—not just the brain talking to the gut, but the gut talking to the brain as well. The gut is where we create cravings, impulses, some addictions, instincts, intuition, and the chemistry of the hormonal communication in the body. The different frequencies or speeds of our brainwaves influence every thought, memory, feeling, idea, action, and sensation we have.

Based on that explanation, and looking to the details of the brainwave diagram, which of these brainwave states do you mostly live?

Assessing brainwave activity is our modern way of assessing or deciding between life and death. For example, life is no longer measured by our beating hearts, or the little "beep... beep... beep..." heard from the monitor of the hospital machinery in a TV medical drama. If we are deemed "brain-dead," it means we have "no discernable brainwaves," and we are then gone, with no hope of return or recovery. That is modern death.

When we are in our waking conscious state, we call it **beta brainwaves**. If you were to look at a visual of the brainwave patterns, you will see beta waves are shown with a very tight, jagged line. That is exactly what the feelings and behaviors are like when we experience the beta state—tight, jagged feelings. We are anxious, and nervous, have heightened senses, and feel like we are waiting for the "other shoe to drop."

Beta is the brainwave we are in most of our conscious time and it's where we make decisions, have willpower, and feel excited, passionate, anxious, or scared. Our fight, flight, or freeze system is in this state, and chronic stress lives here.

If we close our eyes for a few seconds and slow our breath down slightly, we enter **alpha brainwaves**. Taking deeper, slower breaths and becoming aware of our breathing will slow down not only our breath, but also our heartbeat and our blood pressure. An alpha wave is slightly softer than the beta wave, and not quite as jagged. This is true in how it feels as well. Alpha corresponds with feelings of relaxation, reduced anxiety, and happiness—from the release of serotonin to the brain. The alpha state is the beginning of what we traditionally call a state of meditation or hypnosis, where we relax and "let go."

The next brainwave is **theta brainwaves,** which are calmer. This is where the real sweet spot is, in terms of hypnosis or meditation. In this state, the mind can be extremely heightened and acutely aware, even though the body is seriously relaxed. The state of awareness changes and can be very creative. Theta brainwaves are much less jagged and the wave peaks are farther apart than those seen in alpha or beta waves. We may feel "at one" and can have access to deeper levels of the subconscious and unconscious mind. When experiencing theta, some people feel they are "in the zone" and inspired.

Delta brainwaves are the farthest distance apart and have the least jagged waves. Delta waves occur when we are asleep and our brains slow right down. Sleep cycles (going in and out of full delta brainwaves) are about 90 minutes long. Most people experience four or five sleep cycles per night. It is essential to get enough sleep each night, in order to process the day's events in our brain, resolve any issues we have, deposit memories into our memory bank, and repair any damage of our systems an at the cellular level that our bodies require. Sleep needs change over our lifetimes, with older people (in their 70s and 80s) requiring less sleep than younger people. Babies usually sleep for approximately 20 hours per day and teenagers need lots of sleep—around nine hours per night—while going through growth spurts.

During hypnosis or a meditative state, we can achieve alpha and theta brainwaves without reaching delta, or falling asleep. When we hear hypnotists in the movies say "sleep" when hypnotizing, we often assume that the client is asleep, but this is not true. We can access our subconscious, where we visit memories of which our conscious brain is not aware, and we can approach events that cause our thoughts, feelings, and behaviors to occur without our conscious knowledge, because they come from our subconscious mind.

We also now know that the brain sees no difference when either imagining or visualizing, living the real action, or observing the action in a movie or video game. The brain sees it all the same, *especially when there is an emotion attached or an emotion relived along with the imagined experience.* It can be observed as if watching TV, or relived in detail, depending on the intention of recalling the memory. This is why hypnosis can be and often is so effective and so powerful. Through reaching this brainwave and allowing the client to re-experience moments, new perspectives can be examined and accepted allowing healing to take place.

The Brain and the Theory of the Mind: The Conscious Mind (CM)

The structure of the brain is a complex system, yet the brain and the mind are not the same. This is not to start a philosophical discussion about the difference between them, but to open the concepts of the theory of how our mind has developed. Our mind can observe us and our thoughts, from outside ourselves. Our mind serves us—and doesn't—in a variety of ways. The "Theory of the Mind" diagram is meant to explain an understanding of how our mind works. Let's look at that diagram and then discuss the concepts presented in it.

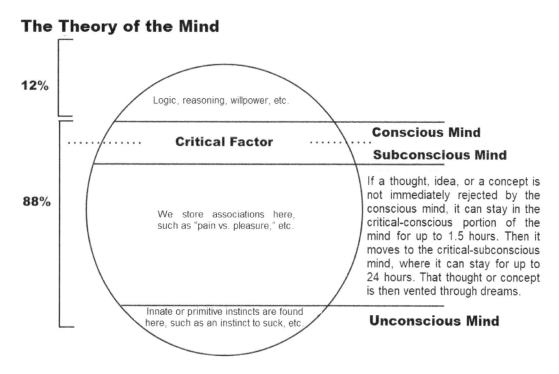

Our conscious mind (CM) makes up approximately 10-12% of our total brain or mind power. Our logical, day-to-day thinking lives in this area of the mind—things of which we are consciously aware. The CM is our general manager but it is just a small part of what is really going on in the whole of our brain.

We think we know what our brain is up to, and we really believe that, but it is important to understand that most of our mind operates below our conscious awareness, and that our brain will do what we tell it to do, whether it is at a conscious or unconscious level. Hence, if our subconscious mind (SCM) is running a program and we are not aware of it, it will produce results that we don't know of—or maybe even want.

This is where the unwanted "bad" habit comes in, for example. Consciously, we don't understand why things happen "to us" or why we do what we do, but the SCM is always attempting to do exactly what we tell it to do. If you don't get what you want in life, the truth is that your subconscious is automatically producing the results and giving exactly what you ask for! Do you truly know what you are asking for? Is your subconscious mind in control of your life? If you are getting results that you want in life, that is great. When you are not getting the results you want, then there is a bug in your programming!

As discussed earlier, it is generally accepted that we *consciously* use about 10-12% of our mind. This seems like a ridiculously small amount, considering how much we handle in our modern lives! The thought of what we are capable of can be overwhelming, especially if we decide to include even a small portion of the other 88-90% of our mind at the conscious level.

The conscious mind is what we use during our normal, waking state of beta brainwaves. This is our normal day-to-day logical, reasoning, problem-solving, and thinking mind. The 10-12% of our CM also includes half of what is called our "Critical Factor" (CF) or the "bouncer" part of the mind. This part of our mind has a memory of about 1.5 hours, so it needs lots of breaks to absorb the unending onslaught of input. Before we look at the "Theory of the Mind" diagram, let's discuss this Critical Factor.

Critical Factor (CF)

The Critical Factor (CF) is a part of the mind that develops near the end of childhood toward adolescence, anywhere from seven to ten or twelve years old. Before then, we accept all input from those around us as the "truth" because we have no adult thinking or decision-making power yet—no critical thought. When we develop a Critical Factor in all areas, we accept or reject new ideas, based on how we were socialized by the adults in our childhood—nature's way of socializing and protecting us. This can be a good thing and a bad thing; depending on the level of education, knowledge, moral fiber, and behavior of the adults in our lives, we will either benefit from this or sometimes be harmed. Whichever is the case, this embedded Critical Factor sifts through all our decision-making. This is largely done at a subconscious level (as well as a conscious level), so we are sometimes even often not even aware of what is happening. This can lead to unconscious reactions and behaviors that can create both small and large difficulties in life.

The Critical Factor is half in our conscious mind and half in our subconscious mind. The critical part of these two minds decides and allows information to seep into our belief system only when it has permission, whether it is close enough to our existing worldview, or whether one changes or reframes the perceptions of the original idea through increased awareness, using meditation or hypnosis.

The Critical Factor part of our mind has been conditioned since we were very young to only accept the ideas and beliefs that we already accept and believe. This is where the expression "you can't teach an old dog new tricks" may come from. Reinforcement of more of the same kind of thinking creates the difference between those of a "fixed mindset" and those who possess a "growth mindset." It can take a huge effort or sometimes even a trauma for us to change our beliefs, reassess them, or be open to a growth mindset.[78]

The Critical Factor part of our brain filters out so much that we don't really have to pay attention to everything. If we were physically able to pay attention to everything in our environment, we would obviously be overwhelmed by too much information. We tend to observe only what we expect.

Our expectations influence our attention, as seen by "the Monkey Business illusion" experiment by David Simon, shown in that short video.[79]

The experiment shows how our attention is programmed in our conscious mind to see what we believe. We have an expression "seeing is believing," but the reality of life is "believing is seeing." This means that we will not even register something that we do not believe. Once we believe it, *then* we can experience it. Our Critical Factor literally bounces ideas from entering if, it is outside our belief system. This is the incredible filtering power of cultural norms, gender roles, stereotypes, training, organized religions, and such.

Subconscious Mind (SCM)

Our subconscious mind (SCM) is the other 88-90% of our mind and contains the other half of the Critical Factor. The subconscious mind is the part that is our "programming." It runs in the background, mostly without our awareness. It is usually only when things are not working that we draw attention to it. If we often wonder why things are NOT going the way we want them to go, it is because the subconscious mind has more control over our activities and habits than our conscious mind does.

Our subconscious or emotional mind includes our primitive brain, which contains our base instinctive reactions, such as the instinct to suck at birth and the fear of loud noises or falling. We are not normally aware of this part of our mind—and with good reason. If we were aware of every function of our brain or mind, we would go crazy!

We don't need to be aware of every heartbeat or breath, or of our liver or blood functions. They just happen, even though our brain is in control, on time, and on schedule. However, we hold memories recorded in our subconscious and we can access them if and when we want to. Memories of everything that we have ever experienced are stored there.

As we grow and develop, our SCM forms our worldview, based on our emotional reactions to events in our lives. Because we are in such a state of suggestibility (theta brainwaves) as infants and children, all the information surrounding us goes straight into our memories with no filters *and* with an emotional attachments.

As we experience life, we sort these things into "positives" and "negatives," based on our emotional reactions to them as emotional beings. These emotional attachments can be thought of as "triggers" that can cause recurring thoughts, feelings, or behaviors at the subconscious level (they happen automatically, without our awareness).

The good part of all of this memory storage is that it *is* there and accessible. However, our memories can be distorted by a lack of critical observation (when we are children). Our worldview can be distorted, and our "programming" may cause us problems later in life. All of this can be held at the subconscious level, meaning we aren't consciously aware of where these thoughts, feelings, and behaviors come from, and all of this can be exacerbated by the lack of a healthy microbiome and the communication between our gut and our brain. Therefore, in order to have optimum brain health, it is extremely important to not only be more aware of our thoughts, feelings, and behaviors, but to ensure our gut and the messaging between our gut and brain are at their optimum performance for the success of our whole and entire being.

The SCM is where all our habits are stored, so that we don't need to be aware of things that we do repeatedly. The upside of this is that it is "God's way" (as someone put it) of making our lives so much easier. These habits are based on our "paradigms" or worldview that forms during our early years and our childhoods, through constant repetition of the ideas and examples of behaviors surrounding us. The downside of this part of our mind is that we create paradigms, of which we are not aware, especially when we find our behavior causes us problems. When we have "things" appear in our lives that we don't like, sheer willpower sometimes cannot change the outcome. Often, we need to change our internal paradigm around that habit, in order to have lasting results. This is difficult to do on our own and is quite difficult—practically impossible—to do in our CM.

How the Theory of the Mind Ties into Brainwaves

Brainwaves actually line up with the Theory of the Mind in the following ways:

Beta brainwaves are most aligned with the CM or conscious mind. This is where we are aware of our logical thoughts, our "will," our willpower, and our high cognitive functioning (our decision-making and problem-solving abilities). The beta state where we do our normal, day-to-day thinking and where we "think things through."

The Critical Factor is our belief system programming, which will bounce ideas that do not fit into our beliefs. We are mostly aware of this, in concept, but not always in detail. For example, we sometimes make logical decisions based on our "gut instinct," which lives in both our SCM or subconscious mind and the "second brain" in our gut.

Alpha brainwaves occur when we begin to access our SCM. We can easily start this brain activity simply by closing our eyes and mindfully watching our breathing. As our breath slows down, all systems in our body slow, including our heart, blood pressure and in sync, brainwaves. All organs in our body ultimately slow, with this decrease in overall activity. In a light state of meditation or trance, we can begin to relax and access feelings of connection.

Relaxing deeper and further through the alpha state, we move into **theta brainwaves** which is where we feel creative, intuitive, and deep emotional connections—to both ourselves and others. We are also more "suggestible" in theta, so this is useful in therapy to be able to approach issues from unusual perspectives.

Total relaxation takes us to **delta brainwaves** or sleep. All mammals (and probably all life on Earth) somehow must sleep or rest between periods of activity, feeding, mating, or other imperative impulses.

The variety in brainwave activity demonstrates that not all human experiences occur at the same brainwaves or with the same level of consciousness. Even though we humans think we operate mostly in our conscious mind awareness, much of what we experience is motivated and occurs below our conscious level (as extensively discussed).

High-impact experiences are attached to emotions and stored not only in our subconscious but also in our bodies. Because of this, events can be more easily remembered when accompanied by an emotion, and the level of the emotion makes a difference to the remembrance. For example, everyone remembers where they were when Kennedy was assassinated (if you are old enough) or when the 9/11 planes struck the World Trade Centre or the joy of being present at the birth of your first child. If we feel shocked, scared, or extreme joy, we remember those events clearly. Being aware of how emotions are remembered and stored in our bodies as well as our minds is another role that the gut-brain connection can be tapped into, to increase health and wellness.

The food-mood connection in this section can be seen through the proactive influence food has on stress, particularly through probiotic and prebiotic functions, to create hormones such as serotonin. When we reduce stress and increase serotonin, our happiness and the control of our emotional state increases. When we learn to operate from the inside out (where we decide and create or respond with our emotions instead of automatically reacting), we find increasing happiness.

Chapter 6—Key Highlights:

1. The human brain is a highly evolved and complex organ.

2. Our conscious mind makes up 10-12% of the brain and the subconscious mind makes up the other 88-90%.

3. Almost ALL human functions occur beneath our conscious awareness. As well, most of our actions and reactions to life happen at the subconscious level, influenced by our emotional brain and the second brain in the gut.

4. Evolution has built several automatic systems in our brains, which allow a quick response to dangers in our environment so we never have to actually think about our reactions.

5. The limbic system forms what is commonly called our fight, flight, or freeze response, and it combines higher mental functions and primitive emotions into one system.

6. The limbic system structures are the amygdala (the emotion centre of the brain), the hippocampus (the memory indexer), and the hypothalamus (which directs a multitude of important functions).

7. We move through four stages, when developing and mastering a new skill: unconscious incompetence, conscious incompetence, conscious competence, and unconscious competence.

8. Stress affects the balance of the microbiome. Stress also inhibits our abilities to focus and learn. Our emotional life, therefore, plays a frontline role in human immunity as well as our mental health.

9. The Vagus nerve is the chief communicator between the gut and brain. Chemical and electrical energies communicate our emotions and feelings throughout our bodies, particularly through the direct connection between the gut and the brain. We use our neurons and our chemistry for communication.

10. Humans experience a variety of brainwaves—gamma, beta, alpha, theta, and delta—which all have different frequencies and purposes. They help us think, feel, behave, move, and process in different ways and at different levels of awareness.

11. Beta waves = feelings of anxiousness; alpha waves = slower breathing and body processes as wells as feelings of relaxation; theta waves = even calmer and the mind is heightened while the body is relaxed; delta = sleep; and gamma = productivity and complex cognitive functions.

12. Meditation and hypnosis have many physical and psychological benefits.

13. The Critical Factor (CF) is a part of the mind that develops near the end of childhood toward adolescence and allows us to accept or reject new ideas. It is half in our conscious mind and half in our subconscious mind.

14. The subconscious mind is the part that is our "programming." It runs in the background, mostly without our awareness, and is the part where memories are stored and accessed. Memories are more easily remembered when accompanied by an emotion.

15. Our minds attach meaning to events and thus create our own perception and experience of reality, based on our worldview and previous experiences.

16. Our brainwaves are under our control. We can access changes in perception, bypassing the Critical Factor (CF) to reach the subconscious mind (SCM). Meditation and hypnosis can access and facilitate this change.

Chapter 7: The Gut-Brain-Microbiome Connection

Our overall health is set through the filter of our perception.

The power of thought-belief-placebo has been well-studied, documented, and repeated scientifically throughout history. "If we believe it, then we see it" is a concept that has been previously discussed, yet still many feel unable or unwilling to open their minds to information beyond their existing mindsets and beliefs—especially in the case of this subject, for those uneducated in nutrition. Even for me, who has an abundance of nutritional education, it has been a long journey. The evidence now has mounted to an undeniable truth: there is a powerful gut-brain connection and the human gut microbiome is much more powerful and in control of our destiny, health, and wellness than we ever thought probable or possible.

Human culture has known for millennia that our gut and brain work together. Both our conscious and unconscious minds assess our environment, to "think things through." Often, the subconscious or unconscious mind is really "feeling things through," using our gut reactions or gut instincts to first assess the person or situation and then make a decision. For example, we sometimes know very quickly if we dislike or trust someone, want to know a person better, hire them, date them, or even marry them.

Recent medical research has greatly expanded our knowledge of the concept of the gut-brain connection. We now know more about the fact that this connection works both ways. For example, the brain has a dramatic influence over the gut, as well as the other way around. This was initially surprising to the medical community, which saw these as totally separate, with the brain being in charge.

Now, we know the gut has power over the brain and can cause havoc, if not nurtured properly. This is seen through the expanse of all sorts of human disease, which we now know starts in the gut and can cause everything from cravings to major illnesses. These communications go through the nervous and endocrine systems. Stimulations are known to go both brain-to-gut and gut-to-brain. Nerves—primarily the Vagus nerve—provide a direct connection between gut and brain. Also, chemical or hormonal stimulation from a variety of organs affects communication—both ways—through the bloodstream.

In our human evolution, it was necessary for the body to favor some systems over others, during certain experiences. For example, we shut down some parts of the gut or the brain to allow another to take over the blood supply, our attention, and be able to react immediately, in times of crisis or emergency. This is meant to be a good thing, imperative for our survival. However, in modern society, this unconscious reaction to stress creates a vicious cycle. Psychological stress can actually increase gut permeability and change the population of the gut bacteria. The imbalance is known as dysbiosis, which leads to increased leakiness of the tight junctions in the gut, ultimately leading to greater inflammation.[80] (We have talked about this before.)

Food, Mood, and Mental Health

Mental health has a long history of stigmatization in human society. Even though there has likely always been mental illness in all cultures, there have been varying degrees of acceptance and treatment. Some cultures forbid showing any weakness, especially regarding mental health concerns. Other cultures may sympathize, to a degree, but asking for help can be difficult and finding it can be even harder. As a result, suicide statistics are at an all-time high. Anxiety and depression medications are often distributed to patients, before any other options. Most often, in our western society, by the time a real problem in mental health is discovered or disclosed, it has grown beyond the point of an easy fix. Typically, medical doctors are involved in treatment and prescription drugs are the norm. This trend to using drugs for treating mental health has led to drug overuse and abuse. Addictions and side effects of medications are also the norm, with little change in the approach. However, these drugs do not make the problem go away, and often, the outcome is having to continue with the prescription for the rest of one's life.

Information on the connection of the gut and brain has been around for many years. It has gone in and out of favor over the last 100 years, since it was first published, causing a new wave of interest in this topic around the world. Being an MD, with specialties in neurology and nutrition, as well as the mother of an autistic child, Dr. Natasha Campbell-McBride was highly motivated to gather together the latest research of the time. Her connection between diet and brain development (with the backdrop of Autism and a mother's motivation) addressed the phenomenon of the huge increase of this condition in various populations. Being so widespread, her mention of "doctors, biochemists, biologists, and simply intelligent human beings as parents, looking for solutions to their child's problems," banded organizations together and may just have been the seed which fueled the interest in the gut-brain connection and the study of the human gut microbiome.[81]

Some of the greatest advances in the last few years in the connection between food and mood (our mental health) have occurred in the research from the Food and Mood Centre at Deakin University, in Australia. Many studies from the Food and Mood Centre—both complete and in progress—point to the increasing evidence that food has direct impact on mood as well as on specific mental health issues.[82]

Food has sometimes been proven to be more impactful than current medications are, and certainly, much better than placebos. Food even changes our DNA! Not only does food influence our physical and mental health, but it also has a direct connection to the health and wellbeing of our microbiota. The microbiota in our GI tract is now seen as a separate "organ," referred to as the "second brain," and has been and is being connected to many and perhaps even all human diseases.

Let's now look at where and how the gut-brain connection affects mental and physical health.

The Gut-Brain Connection affects Mental Health:

a) Anxiety and Depression

It is common to suffer from both anxiety and depression at the same time, but not always. Sometimes, persistent anxiety is what leads to depressive symptoms. The chief difference between the two is that anxiety is characterized by fear, apprehension, nervous thoughts, and exaggerated worries about the future. Depression doesn't entail such fears. Depression revolves around a sense of hopelessness—the sky has already fallen, life is bad, and nothing can go right.

Anxiety and depression are often cached together because they are related psychologically and have many similar physical symptoms (negative thinking, headaches, pain, nausea, and GI problems).

Depression and anxiety both suffer disruption of the gut microbiota. Numerous studies have found the same kinds of features in those with anxiety disorder as in those with depression: higher levels of gut inflammation, higher levels of systemic inflammation, lower levels of BDNF (brain's growth hormone), higher levels of cortisol, over-reactive stress responses, and an increased permeability of the gut.

While the research is still in its infancy, it has become clear that anxiety disorders and depression are caused by a combination of factors that most definitely include the state and function of the gut and its inhabitants. Further studies recognized that it was not enough to feed the subjects just probiotics, but the probiotics must be fed as well.

Adding food for the "good bacteria" in the form of probiotic or specific fiber resulted in good psychological changes. The underlying theory was that if you're anxious to begin with, you'll be more reactive to negativity as well as emotionally-charged images and/or words. Subjects who increased their consumption of prebiotics foods (high fiber) and paid more attention to positive information had less anxiety with negative stimuli, plus lower levels of cortisol.[83] These results are similar to individuals on antidepressants. Other research relates the microbiota of the intestine with diseases of the nervous system and its possible treatment through use of good bacteria. Indeed, although probiotic bacteria will be concentrated after ingestion, mainly in the intestinal epithelium (where they provide the host with essential nutrients and modulation of the immune system), there is evidence they may also produce neuroactive substances which act on the brain-gut axis. This is great news for those wanting to solve the original problems rather than just treating symptoms with pharmaceuticals.[84]

b) Attention Deficit Disorder (ADD) and Attention Deficit Hyperactivity Disorder (ADHD)

Since 1990, there has been a dramatic increase in a myriad of brain disorders (ADD, ADHD, Autism spectrum, Asperger's, MS, Parkinson's, and Alzheimer's), which has changed the landscape of what it means to grow up in North America. Not only is there a huge increase in the expression of the Autism spectrum since the 1990s, but we know now that the gut has a huge connection to imbalances in the brain. For example, the prevalence of constipation is three times higher in kids with ADHD, indicating that something is going on in the GI of these children.[85] In Germany, researchers revealed a high gluten sensitivity in children with ADHD—more common than the rest of the population, which is already high. Removing gluten from the diets of ADHD patients and children with Autism reported a significant improvement in behavior and functioning than before the period of switching to a gluten-free diet.[86] This research proves that the gut (and what we eat) affects the brain.

Probiotics are known to boost one's cognitive function.[87] Specific varieties and species are now being studied, to test the different strains out for demonstration to support different issues or symptoms in the brain's functions.

Gamma aminobutyric acid (GABA) is largely deficient in the brains of children who have ADHD. GABA is essential to and assists in calming the brain and body, and supports sleep and relaxation. Zinc and vitamin B6 are sources for the chemistry basics needed to create GABA, which means that either the body is unable to extract those nutrients in children with ADHD, or that they are not sufficiently present in their diets.

Those two ingredients can come from common food. Specific types of *Lactobacillus* and *Bifidobacterium* produce GABA in abundance.[88] As mentioned in Chapter 5, foods that contain these include kimchi, sauerkraut, pickles, yogurt, kefir, seaweed, and miso soup. Research is underway to discover the specifics of the species and varieties of bacteria whose presence in the gut made improvements in mood and memory, a decrease in anxiety, and more.

Technology use and frequency increases the incidence of brain issues such as ADD and ADHD. An increase in screen time—via televisions or computer screens (for watching shows or movies, doing reading or research, and/or playing video games)—appears to increase feelings of disconnection, stress, and also GI issues. With less face-to-face time and human connection, our ability to self-regulate and have real emotional connections decrease.

Facial cues, voice inflections, and other body language are keys to understanding each other. Human communication is 80% physical. Only 20% is based on spoken and written words. If we can't see each other or feel our connections and warmth from another human, miscommunication is often inevitable.

With the focus on technology in forward-thinking education systems and schools, frankly, this direction forces us all to take pause.

Although we understand technology is absolutely essential in our society and economics of the future, the effects of overuse are clear and stand as warnings for boundaries and controls in our homes, schools, and workplaces. This applies to both adults and children. Because of the huge increase in technology in schools and workplaces, this stacks up to create ongoing stress in communication and therefore, our relationships.

c) Autism

Autism is growing at a remarkable rate in western societies. Since 2004, it grew from one child in 166 to one in 59 children in the U.S., and it shows no signs of slowing down.[89] Predictions indicate that this trend will have a massive drain on healthcare in the future, with respect to the education and care of those children.

It is well-known that most children with Autism also suffer from digestive disorders, including abdominal pain, constipation, diarrhea, bloating. Many studies now show that GI conditions are among the hallmarks of Autism.[90] Autistic people are three-and-a-half times more likely to have chronic diarrhea and constipation than their peers.

No two individuals are exactly alike and there are now 70 million people worldwide who are recognized in the Autism spectrum. New suspicions about the autistic disorder include the possibility that Autism isn't usually inherited, even when it runs in families. Legitimate studies from top institutions are currently uncovering the gut-brain connection to this disorder. Gut bacteria are connected to brain development, and deficiencies in them may contribute to the development and progression of the long-term effects of the brain disorder.[91]

A leaky gut, an overly-active immune response, and general inflammation that reaches the brain are among the many hallmarks of recognizing Autism now. Not surprisingly, many experts currently recommend a gluten-free and sugar-free diet for those with Autism. Autistic people also tend to have higher levels of the clostridial species in the gut, which tends to crowd out the balancing effects of other gut bacteria.[92] This can be due to the higher levels of sugar found in an untreated autistic person's gut, their carbohydrate cravings, and the like. Refined sugar is a known fuel for clostridium (intestinal bacteria that thrive in the absence of oxygen).

The Gut-Brain Connection affects Physical Health:

d) Immunity

It has been mentioned before that immunity is directly connected to the inoculation of the gut microbiota through a normal, healthy, *timely,* natural birth. When a baby passes through the vaginal canal, the health of the mother's bacterial culture implants the lifelong health of her baby while passing through. If born via a Caesarian section, the baby becomes inoculated with cells from the operating room, including skin and other cells from the surgical team, the mother, father, and others in the scrubbed room.

This inoculation prepares the infant's entire digestive system to have the ability to digest breast milk. The breast milk ingredients then prepare the gut for other ingested foods, as child development occurs. When babies are born without this preparation for the child's life, it starts a cascade of events that may incur infections (such as throat or ear infections), precipitating the use and overuse of antibiotics. This launch is anything but healthy for the child's life and sets patterns that can last a lifetime.

Studies have shown that babies born by C-section have a higher incidence of immunity problems, develop more diseases and allergies, and are more prone to obesity later in life. The cause appears to be the lack of a proper transfer of the gut microbiota. Also included in this research is the discovery of the inclusion of foodstuffs in breast milk that have nothing to do with the feeding of the baby. Infants cannot digest it. This discovery has set a myriad of assumptions about the meaning of health for infants. This revelation has shocked the medical community and emphasized the magnitude of importance to have a vaginal birth and successful breastfeeding. We knew it was important, but we now know how important it really is. This is the first real evidence that these natural processes are essential for human growth and development as well as for a healthy life thereafter. There is also increasing evidence that the timing of gestation accompanies a timing of vaginal microbiome development, so that both come together to be of the best benefit for the newborn's success.

e) Obesity and Type 2 Diabetes

"Eat less, move more" has been the byline of the diet and weight loss industry as long as can be remembered. Even in my university education, we were taught that an energy balance the secret to weight management—calories in versus calories out. Science has now shown that this is not true. In fact, it is quite far from the truth. The gut community of lean people represents a "rainforest-like" entity, filled with many species.

The gut community of obese people is much less diverse. We used to think that being overweight or obese was a math problem—a factor of excess caloric intake compared to calories expended. New research has revealed that the microbiome plays a fundamental role in our body's energy dynamics, which affects the calories consumed versus the calories burned equation. If you house too many types of bacteria that can more efficiently remove calories from food, you'll absorb more than you need, leading to fat promotion and storage.

Obesity is an inflammatory disease (just like brain diseases are). Obesity seems to be related to the gut microbiome in the balance between two specific classes of bacteria (Firmicutes and Bacteroidetes), which are directly related to the balance in the microbiome. In fact, studies with twins have shown that the real culprit of weight gain could very well be our microbes because those two groups of bacteria make up about 90% of our microbial population.

Firmicutes are commonly referred to as bad gut microbes, due to their negative influence on glucose and fat metabolism. Bacteroidetes perform essential metabolic conversions, such as degradation of proteins or complex sugar polymers. An increased ratio of Firmicutes to Bacteroidetes species has been correlated with obesity and Type 2 Diabetes. It also appears that a higher concentration of Firmicutes is strongly associated with increased inflammation.

Studies have shown that this population can be dramatically altered by increasing the fiber content of our diet. Also, according to one Harvard study, our western guts are dominated by Firmicutes, and Africans' by Bacteroidetes, which shows a direct correlation between the obesity results in the respective populations. Firmicutes bacteria are exceptionally adept at extracting calories from food, causing an increase in caloric absorption and thus, enabling an increased fat storage ability.

The Firmicutes to Bacteroidetes ratio is now identified as an "obesity marker" in gut populations. These populations can be influenced and monitored, which means that there could be a distinct possibility to help those who are chronically obese avoid looking at dangerous bypass surgeries as their magic bullet.

Insulin Resistance → Diabetes

Our western diet is almost exclusively based on carbohydrates for fuel. As a result, our bodies are in a constant process of eating, breaking down, and absorbing sugar into our bloodstream. Since the 1970s and 1980s, and especially since Canada's Food Guide inception, there has been a conscious and considerable effort towards reduction in fat consumption—not carbohydrates or sugar. Erroneous information taught during those times deterred consumption of fats, due to a fear of coronary and pulmonary diseases and the fact that fat has twice the number of calories as carbohydrates. It was also thought that fat clogs arteries. The result of this information has been generations of people avoiding fats, eating a low-fat diet, and the food industry replacing fat with sugar in many processed foods. It turns out that fat is not the enemy; sugar is.[93]

Insulin is one of the body's main hormones and plays a main role in our metabolism. Our body produces insulin to enable us to extract sugar from our blood so that we can use the energy. Our cells can only accept glucose with the help of insulin, which acts like a transporter.

Insulin helps us facilitate energy from our food into our cells so we can create energy. When normal and healthy, a cell has abundant receptors for insulin, and has no problem responding to it. When a cell is mercilessly exposed to high levels of insulin through a never-ending presence of glucose, caused by consuming too many carbohydrates and refined sugars, the cell does something brilliant to adapt—it reduces the number of insulin-responsive receptors on its surface. Unfortunately, this ultimately causes the cell to become resistant to insulin.

Once a cell is insulin-resistant, it's unable to take glucose from the blood, thus leaving glucose in the bloodstream. Once the cell is insulin-resistant, as with most biological processes, there is a "fail-safe" backup system in place, because the body doesn't want glucose lingering in the blood. It tells the pancreas to increase the amount of insulin to mop up the glucose, which it does. Thus, higher and higher levels of insulin are needed because the cells aren't as responsive to insulin. This ultimately results in Type 2 Diabetes.

At the 2014 Harvard symposium on microbiomes, Dr. Max Nieuwdorp, from the University of Amsterdam's Faculty of Medicine, presented his findings on studying obesity and Type 2 Diabetes.[94]

He transplanted healthy fecal matter from lean, non-diabetic mice into diabetic mice and the results were astounding. The mice who had the transplant reversed their Diabetes! The question he posed from this research was: "What if we owe our obesity challenges to a sick and dysfunctional congregation of intestinal bugs?" Even in the case of the very controversial gastric surgery, where obese people have their "stomachs stapled," it was generally thought (in the early stages of this procedure) that the stapling process worked because of eating less. Now, there is evidence that the process actually changes the gut microbiota.

Exercise studies now show that increases in Bacteroidetes and reductions in Firmicutes result in weight loss or management, so exercising and increasing fiber should reduce weight. By changing your gut microbiota (through eating healthier foods), obesity and Type 2 Diabetes can be avoided and you will feel better.

The Gut-Brain Connection and Energy in the Body

Stress, trauma, grief, and fear have an emotional impact and get caught in our bodies energetically. Ancient civilizations knew this, and traditional Ayurvedic and Chinese medicine still use this knowledge in their practices. Science is catching up with these ancient practices and measurements can now be taken with technological tools that are able to measure energy fields, transfers of energy, brainwaves, and more.

When we pay attention to the feelings we get when imagining our traumatic events, we can often associate them with an area or particular body parts where the emotion lives. We can also infer other properties to these emotions—colors, textures, temperatures, etc.—which enhance our perception and interpretation of their meaning, beginnings, and cascading effects.

Emotional experiences can be stored in particular places in our bodies according to the type of emotion, from joy and bliss all the way down the emotional ladder to sadness, fear, grief, depression, and despair.

Emotional trauma migrates to certain areas of the body, where specific diseases are precipitated.

Through experience with thousands of clients, well-known and respected practitioners, such as Louise Hay, found similar emotional afflictions seemed to be associated with certain parts of the body.[95] For example, things associated with lower parts of the body (lower legs, knees, feet, and toes) could be related to the fear of moving forward. As one moves in the world using those body parts, grief could be rooted in a lung disease, etc. This tendency was seen again and again in Hay's clients, to the point where she documented it in several ways, including books, movies, and other documents, many of them entitled *"You Can Heal Your Body."*

So, how can we change our thoughts and feelings, and therefore, our behaviors? Emotional energy can be identified and released from the body in many ways. Ancient methods, fairly well-accepted in western society, include physical techniques such as acupuncture, acupressure, Reiki, and a variety of massage therapies.

Mental therapies such as meditation and hypnosis (using regression therapy, in particular) can also be used to great success.

In the past, shock therapy was used in cases of extreme mental illness. Modern technologies, including Virtual Reality tools, are now showing much promise, because these programs use a similar regression technique of a computer program instead of utilizing one's own visualization creation to recreate and resolve/dissolve emotional issues and trauma.

Also, methods such as EFT (Emotional Freedom Technique or Tapping) have received a lot of attention for success both in mainstream media and the scientific press. Through using such techniques, we access our nervous system and ease the emotional stress that we feel in the body. This is especially useful when individuals feel the need for relief in times of extreme stress and overwhelm. It can also be incorporated as a practice to prevent a build-up of emotional stress and can be "scripted" to deal directly with any personal stressor.

Emotional Freedom Technique (EFT) or Tapping

Dawson Church[96], Nick Ortner[97], and Gary Craig[98] are well-known EFT experts in the international tapping community.

The basic premise of the emotional freedom technique is that one "taps" certain defined energy points on the body (acupressure points and energy meridians) with their fingertips while repeating phrases using themes and wording that emphasize the following:

1. First, accept the feelings and internal conflict, fear, guilt, etc. that one is feeling around a certain decision or behavior. While expressing fear and apprehension, also move toward the expression of the love and acceptance of yourself, wherever you are. This briefly acknowledges the problem and registers it in mind and body.

2. Second, move from your current feelings with acceptance of them towards full expression of the growth you want. Keep expressing the acceptance of yourself and ask for the growth you anticipate by using repeated phrases.

3. Third, acknowledge the growth you want and make it fun, light, in your best interests, and within your grasp.

4. Fourth, emphasize the joy in your results and the joy and fun you feel in the journey *en route* to your results. Acknowledge and create the feelings wanted in the end result. Fully emphasize that feeling and intensify it, as much as possible.

5. Repeat the love and acceptance of yourself through this process.

While you begin speaking, being tapping. Tap all of the points on your body, as labeled in the diagram, in this order: the crown of your head, your eyebrow, the side of your eye, below your eye, below your nose, below your mouth, your collarbone, and your underarm.

EMOTIONAL FREEDOM TECHNIQUE TAPPING POINTS

Speak and tap concurrently. Using the pointer and middle fingers of either (or both) hands, tap on the labelled tapping points while the particular exercise is being recited aloud.

An interesting test to take on your own is to evaluate your level of discomfort and fear *before the exercise* and then re-evaluate it *after the exercise,* to really assess your level of change.

Tapping exercises access our energy meridians and can assist us in being able to release our own trapped emotions and energies. When these things cause disease or discomfort, or worse, debilitations, anything we can do ourselves is a great thing. Much research has been done on this method as well and is worth exploring.

Nick Ortner has a great YouTube tapping demonstration video.[99] The video offers a full demonstration of how to use the EFT.

In this chapter, the food-mood connection is direct and clear. Many mental health issues are proven to be connected to foodstuffs, dietary and fitness habits, stress levels, and general emotional health. The brain and "second brain" (our gut microbiome) communicate directly back and forth, and affect each other through food and brain activity. Cravings of food or other choices come from emotions or your subconscious brain as well as your nervous system. Your emotional health comes through a physical and mental mind-body phenomenon that you can directly change through your habits of thinking and eating. Changing your thoughts and energy can change your feelings—and your resulting behaviors and habits.

Chapter 7—Key Highlights:

1. Our perception of life events is based on our worldview, which is developed before adolescence.

2. Our emotions start in our brain, based on our worldview assessment, and then manifests as a feelings in our body.

3. Gut health and brain health support one another.

4. Our gut-brain health affects many expressions of our health, including mood, mental health (anxiety, depression, Autism, ADD, and ADHD), and physical health (immunity, obesity, and Type 2 Diabetes).

5. Energy is trapped in certain patterns in the body but we can use energetic tools to move or release those trappings. The EFT is a great one to use.

Chapter 8: Environments and Microbes

Just as the Internal Environment (meaning our mental, physical, emotional, and spiritual health) is inside our bodies, the Near Environment is defined as what is immediately outside our bodies (our immediate environment) and how it contributes to our health and wellness. The Near Environment includes things that we have direct contact with—basics such as food, clothing, and shelter—but also includes our interpersonal relationships, what we normally do and have in our day-to-day lives, how we get around, and how we experience the world and its situations. These are complex ideas that involve complex relationships. However, the Near Environment is more anthropological, because we are interacting with things immediately around us.

Human Ecological Model: The Near Environment

Referring back to the Human Ecological Model from Chapter 3, this important Near Environment consists of our close relationships with our home, our friends, our family, and our school and/or work lives. Each of those relationships are comprised of many individuals, their perspectives, and their opinions. The Near Environment also includes how we obtain our food, what types we obtain and how they are grown; what kind of clothing we make, buy, or recycle (or not); and how the fiber of our clothing is raised or manufactured. Additionally, the Near Environment includes transportation and how we arrive at all those places we go in a day; and what it's like immediately around us, in terms of safety, cost, viability, and more. How well we live, how we work and play, our immediate surroundings, our air, surfaces, and the type, accessibility, and safety of the buildings and landscape where we live and work are all included here as well.

In terms of relationships, it is said that the five or six main people in your life influence and create the person you become. Those five or six people support the formation of our beliefs and ideas—our "worldview" (as discussed in the formation of our Conscious Mind and Critical Factor). This is most true from birth to young adolescence (10-12 years old), where the beliefs of those around us become our solid belief system. This belief system becomes the foundation upon which we make most of our decisions for the rest of our lives.

This concept also works deeper and is more complicated than that. Business school professor David Burkus wrote a book called *Friend of a Friend…: Understanding the Hidden Networks That Can Transform Your Life and Your Career*,[100] which shows that not only are we influenced by people we know directly, but also by the friends of our friends. Each person's view, and even their weight and happiness, are affected by friends of friends. These people and their views "normalize" a larger body size as well as a mood uplift or downturn, and certainly the "birds of a feather flock together" saying is true.

Our social networks are very important to our quality of life, our mood, and ultimately, our mental health. This is true for friends, but also school and business colleagues and marriage partners. If we are not happy in our jobs or marriage, or with the people we work with, then going to work, home, or school becomes a chore. Anxiety develops if anything is not working well. Finding our happy place to live and work can be a lifelong project for some, and many people get stuck in roles that are not supportive because of the trap of needing the job, the house, the car, the marriage, etc. There are literally thousands of books on this topic. Finding the right school, job, doctor, therapist, and all of the people we need in our lives to help us thrive is important. However, it need not be difficult, if you know what you need and therefore, what you are looking for.

The Near Environment is also directly connected to our experience of nature. We are really lucky in Canada, particularly in my city of Vancouver. We have nature right outside our doors every morning and we can experience forests, the oceanside, and even wilderness in under an hour—sometimes right inside the city!

Lately, there has been a lot of interest and focus on extreme weather occurrences and climate change. These basic foundations of the Near Environment have a huge effect on a person's life and the culture created, whether one is involved in the creation of the weather and climate or not. For example, to illustrate the idea of us all being interconnected, a poor person living in low-lying Bangladesh, who has never and will never own or drive a car (and maybe even never take a train) will be among the first nations to experience dramatic flooding from climate change, due to the location and elevation of their low-lying Near Environment—the landscape. The same is true for all the island nations of the world.

Human Ecological Model: The Distal Environment

The Distal Environment represents our relationships with overarching structures of society and institutions, the systems within, and the governments and policies—all which set the framework for how we live, work, and play. Those structures set the economy, healthcare, laws, and policies in education and all levels of government, and affect physical infrastructures such as transportation and landscape around cities and rural areas.

These frameworks determine how our overall systems operate, regarding the legal and moral set-up of food and water systems, other natural resources, ethical trades, and more. All of the esoteric decisions and policy models create the foundations for how society will function and flow, as well as how we develop our lives, families, and communities within them to create the most opportunities for health and success. These Distal Environment connections are ones that are least visible to us but are, in fact, more important than we realize, because they create the boundaries for the frameworks within which we must work to achieve our life goals.

The weather and climate are affected greatly by the amount of care we take with our governmental and international decisions around economic and climate change impact. These decisions include those around food system policies, rural and urban planning, world trade, and stewardship of the Earth, at all levels of government, from household and civic to national and international agreements. All of these decisions are made by people for the people of the world.

The terrible bush fires in Alberta, British Columbia, California, Amazon, and Australia and their devastation effects on forests, wildlife, individual family homes, and communities have been extremely traumatizing for many people in the world. Flooding and oceans rising (due to the effects of climate change) are very worrisome to those living on coastlines or islands.

As environments change, we see new diseases and contagions emerge, and one-celled organisms evolve the fastest. The current Novel Coronavirus (COVID-19) pandemic is an extreme example of how our lives can change drastically and instantly, on a global level. The recent global reaction to police brutality in the George Floyd incident in the U.S. is an example of how the motivated citizens of the world can make societal change happen quickly if we want to. We are all collectively becoming increasingly concerned about the future of life on our planet. We must take these fearful and catastrophic images and use them as a catalyst to bring ourselves together and make better decisions for ourselves, future generations, and our planet.

What Kills Beneficial Microbiomes?

Back in the times before refrigeration, we brought food into our homes and we had to decide on its best storage because fresh foods would spoil quickly. We developed many ways of food preservation over the millennia. From pits in the Earth to clay jars, bottles sealed with lead or wax, salting, freezing, dehydrating, cooking, and adding sugar or vinegar, we have used everything to preserve food. It is even suspected by archeologists that humans invented agriculture—not because we wanted to grow grain to eat as bread, but because we wanted to make alcohol! Wine and beer are said to have been developed because of difficulties accessing clean water, especially when travelling to battles.

Over time, we kept food outside in the winter to chill (freezing and chilling), we dried it in the sun and wind (dehydration), hung it over the fire and in the rafters to dry out (smoking), added salt to meat, to draw out the water, which would support bacterial growth (salting and curing), added salt and buried it in the ground to "rot" (fermentation or pickling), stored liquids in barrels or cisterns (fermentation of beer and wine), and left it on the counter too long (fermented milk/kefir, yogurt, and fermented vegetables). All of these methods allowed the extension of the life of palatable and nutritious foods. Since modern refrigeration, these methods have declined and most food in modern North American society is stored for the short term in the refrigerator—reducing the fermentation process and reducing our intake of fermented foods, in general.

Many cultures knew the value of these foods and their anecdotal, longevity-promoting benefits. Some left bread to dry, for eating later on ships, or let it go moldy, for medicinal purposes. However, not until recent times has the scientific community recognized the intrinsic value and even the necessity of these transformative foods in our human diet. It seems we actually do need them for us to be healthy and disease-free. Not only have we evolved as a species, but we have co-evolved with our food, as it spoils, along with the intrinsic microbes certain foods carry.

Chemicals

About 100 years ago, chemistry as a way to improve our lives became a focus of research and development. There were many factors involved in this push, including warfare and the precipitating pharmaceutical and agricultural chemicals resulting from it.

A focus on chemical warfare started and was toxic during WWI (World War I), and many people were killed or suffered the consequences of being exposed to the chemicals used in trench warfare. Chemical warfare was inexpensive, fast, and deadly to humans and animals. At the end of the war, there were stockpiles of nerve agents (chemicals). Chemical warfare techniques continued on during WWII (World War II), and at that time, the growth of petroleum products took off (during the late 1940s and early 1950s), as did the evolution of chemical-killing agents. That period marked the beginning of the development of chemical agents in farming, when petroleum chemicals were left over after wars.

During the Vietnam War, "Agent Orange" was dumped by the ton on the forests of North Vietnam to reduce foliage cover and expose Viet Cong snipers. Such exfoliants and defoliants are chemicals that were used to gradually exterminate the enemy were also developed into herbicides, pesticides, and insecticides that are used today.

In conjunction with those chemical plant and animal killers, the development of Genetically Modified Foods (GMOs) has evolved. Today, commodity crops worldwide (such as wheat, corn, and soy) are now almost all grown from genetically-modified seeds, which are resistant to the herbicide *glyphosate*. (Roundup is the brand name for this herbicide, which is the most widely used herbicide in the United States.) GMO plants are created resistant to the spraying agent, so the plant survives, but the weeds, which can inhibit growth of the GMO, are killed. Thus, the commodity crops of GMO wheat, corn and soy, in particular, are laden with pesticides, and are in all levels of food processing in our society, from flour and cornstarch to mixes, sauces, salad dressings, and canned, frozen, or boxed foods.

One of the traits of GMO plants is that the seeds create plants that do not create flowers or seeds themselves. This results in a closed loop with the suppliers, and farmers are faced with two major problems with this development. First, if the plants do not create seeds, farmers must keep buying more of those seeds. Thus, it is impossible to collect seeds from the crops and replant for free (as man has done since the beginning of agriculture). Farmers are now beholden to the developers of the "patented" GMO seeds. This also means that all the way up and down the food chain, this chemical is insidious in our food. Second, the seeds produce plants that are resistant to herbicides, so they can survive the spraying of chemicals that kill the weeds. This means that every farmer that uses GMO seeds will, by definition, use spraying to eliminate weeds. Therefore, almost none of the world's commodity crops are now grown organically. This is not a very good thing.

Glyphosate was thought to be safe for humans... until recently. At the time of glyphosate development, we did not know anything about the human gut microbiome. Now, we do. Now, we know that glyphosate destroys microbes in the soil, the air, the water, and in our gut. I just read about a class action lawsuit recently—the Roundup Weed Killer Lawsuit.[101] Glyphosate is now beginning to emerge as a huge participant in the health crisis of the developed world, namely in Leaky Gut Syndrome, inflammation, increases in obesity, mental health issues (including anxiety and depression), auto-immune diseases, and cancer.

Big Agra

"Big Agra" is a term that refers to the highly-mechanized and chemically-laden process of agriculture, as it is today. No longer are there thousands of small family farms that existed and were part of the food system that our grandparents experienced.

After the two World Wars, the farming industry became more and more "big business," particularly as smaller farms were bought up and formed into the gigantic tracks of mono-cultured crops that we see in North America today. Much of the agriculture in North America is controlled and owned by only a few large companies.[102] Over time, they have consolidated into larger and larger companies—entities that become the only ones who can afford to be competitive in the global marketplace.

Depleted Soil

As aforementioned, the active ingredient in the weed killer called Roundup is glyphosate, which has long been promoted as "safe" for use on plants in the food supply. What has been discovered is that glyphosate kills microbes in the soil. It may also kill microbial life on the surface of the plants, as this is a brand new area of research and we truly don't know for sure what the entire impact is or will be. Soil also has a microbiome that differs in various parts of the world, and many species of soil microbes are going extinct, along with the millions of other life forms, which are currently under pressure.

Food no longer has the same nutritional values as when our grandparents lived,[103] and it's a two-edged sword. Plants may have extreme difficulty absorbing nutrients without the help of the microbes, just as we do! It makes perfect sense that if soil does not have the proper nutrients, plants cannot absorb them. If microbes in the soil perform the same kind of functions (transfers, extraction, and enhancement) as those who populate our gut, then the fruit or vegetable cannot properly absorb whatever is present in the soil.

Big Pharma

"Big Pharma" is an expression used to describe the smaller number of larger companies that control the pharmaceutical industry in North America. This industry promotes and creates a "need" that directly influences the health of humans and the domestic animal population. The overuse of antibiotics for the last 50 years has been identified and recently, steps have been made to deter such drug overuse.

Emphasis in this industry is on using drugs, above all else, to fix health problems. In doing this, pharmaceutical companies have utilized and administered such large amounts of antibiotics and other drugs that they are now present in every water resource in the North American continent. Levels of drugs are now found in every environment, waterway, and water supply, etc.

With the overuse of antibiotics comes the fear that medicine cannot keep ahead of all the resistant bacteria created. As a result of "preventative antibiotics" use, many of our farm animals are sick and our water supply is polluted.

Polluted Air and Water

Pollution of air and water can extend from the pharmaceutical industry's influence above to the feces-infested runoff water from cattle, pork, and chicken feedlots. Using "preventative antibiotics" in farming is now a normal procedure in North America. Water sources become polluted from industrial agriculture, and people living near big agricultural lots complain of smells as well as fecal matter pollution in creeks, streams and estuaries.[104]

Cleaning Supplies

One of the current culprits contributing to chemicals in the Near and Distal Environments is the category of household cleaning. Because we have been brainwashed into disinfecting everything constantly, from our hands to our floors, we have overused heavy chemicals in our homes and gardens. We have done this to the point where our good bugs are suffering or are gone.

We can see this in the huge increase of disease in our culture, especially with allergies and sensitivities. When a bit of soap and water, baking soda, or vinegar would do, we instead used the "big guns" of bleach and other chemicals—unnecessarily. A study in Sweden discovered that people who use regular dish soap and hot water to wash their household dishes had much stronger levels of immunity, fewer allergies, and more good bacteria in their gut than those who regularly used dishwashing machines.[105]

The food-mood connection in this chapter is clear. Part of our mental health depends on the foods we consume, and foods depend on many factors all around the circle of the Human Ecological Model. Our Near Environment (our day-to-day surroundings) is most likely to be the source of our personal choices and habits. However, the infrastructure that creates those choices is where the big decisions are made.

Because our entire environmental surroundings have drastically changed in the last 100 years, it is imperative that any education in this area look at the whole problem— the Distal Environment. Hence, the "holistic approach" to understanding the gut-brain-microbiome relationship.

Chapter 8—Key Highlights:

1. Our immediate Near Environment has a big impact on our lives because it includes things that we connect with on a day-to-day basis, such as people, places, and things we can physically see, hear, touch, and emotionally feel. "Food, clothing, and shelter" come to mind as a phrase that lives here.

2. The Distal Environment connects us to the more esoteric infrastructure and framework of our society, institution, and systems of our government.

3. Systems and infrastructure of the Distal Environment set up the policies and settings that the Near Environment works within. Therefore, have a huge impact on what, how, and why we are able to operate as individuals, families, and communities of all sizes.

4. The health of the whole system is set by policies and guidelines within the infrastructure of the Distal Environment as well as the habits and performance of the individuals in the Near Environment.

5. Environmental factors created by institutions and infrastructures put a heavy pressure on microbial life.

6. Chemical pollution from Big Agra, Big Pharma, and more, have depleted our soil as well as contaminated our water and air microbes.

7. All environments have been depleted or contaminated so much in the last 100 years that we need a drastic change in the entire system in order to regain health of not just humans, but all creatures of the planet as well and the Earth itself.

Chapter 9: How to Care For and Support Your Microbiome

What can we do to care for and support our microbiomes? There are three things we can do: use natural and non-toxic cleaning supplies, buy locally, and eat probiotically.

Let's look at each of those recommendations in detail.

1: Use Natural and Non-Toxic Cleaning Supplies

Nowadays, there are many choices in most supermarkets for common household cleaning and beauty products. These range from hand soap, shampoo and conditioner to bathroom, toilet, and oven cleaners. From dishwashing soap, laundry soap, and stain removers to glass and furniture cleaners, there are more and more on the market daily.

Through the power of the Internet, free recipes abound to allow industrious home chemists the chance to "do it yourself"! There has been a movement afoot for years to replace chemicals, namely parabens, in many beauty products. It has long been known that humans absorb many good as well as harmful chemicals through the skin and we use a multitude of products daily.[106]

Our grandmothers had it right when they used a few basic elements to create home recipes for all of these products. A hundred years ago, most women knew how to make many essential household products including basic soap (from fats and ash or lye). Using soap plus Borax, baking soda, lemon juice, vinegar, and other common home ingredients, women made everything from toothpaste to floor cleaner.

For example, vinegar and water is a great cleaning agent for almost anything except stone countertops. (Vodka can be substituted). Lemon can be rubbed on a cutting board to clean it; vinegar and a drop of soap in a cup helps loosen the mess in the microwave; and baking soda, salt, and basic dishwashing soap can handle most household cleaning needs.

In essence, such natural cleaners are not "carpet bombs" on microbial life, like some of the common harsh chemicals can be. When we use harsh chemicals on the bad bugs, the good bugs get hit as well. When we expose our bare skin, chemicals are detrimental to us when touching our hands, face, and scalp. When using these mixtures, we should prepare properly, protecting ourselves with clothing, aprons, gloves, and goggles.

If you need to use harsh chemicals such as bleach, ensure all labels and safety instructions are read and understood. Wear some type of breathing apparatus (such as a mask) and gloves to diminish potential harm. Do not pour harsh ingredients down the drain or outside. Do not mix different chemical mixtures together, either, because the chemistry of combining can cause extreme reactions in gases, foaming, spraying up, or explosions.

2: Buy Locally

One of the best ways we can support the health of the environment is to buy locally. This pertains to all things, but especially food. Buying locally is generally accepted to be within a 100+ mile radius of home.[107] Even within 500 miles could be considered local, in the grand scheme. Within this area, whatever radius, transport of food is much less expensive and has a much lighter carbon footprint. Not only do we support local farmers and markets when we buy local produce and products, but we improve our food security by keeping those brave people in business. This is perhaps the most important point, because it is very difficult to make money farming and we (obviously) need food grown. Also, it is much easier on the environment when we don't spend oil and gas to ship food long distances by trains, planes, and automobiles or trucks. Imagine the difference in price between buying something in Nova Scotia, like local fish or lobster, and the carbon footprint of shipping it live, by airplane, to expensive restaurants in Tokyo. Given a choice, it is always wiser to buy something with less shipping involved. There will always be a market for lobster, but the *real cost* is much more than the customer is paying for it when you include the carbon costs to the environment.

Having your own backyard garden is ideal, of course. Living in Canada, above the forty-ninth parallel, we have a fairly short growing season. There is no way we can grow all the food our population needs here, but the more we can produce locally, the better off we are.

Lately, there has been a large increase in innovative greenhouse production, but this has its own issues with land use, agricultural reserve, and bird safety, at the heart.[108] We are not all living in communities where gardens are possible, but for those interested, community gardens, container gardens, and rooftop gardens can offer a small foray into growing food that can ease some pressure on the locally grown food supply.

Support your local growers as much as you can, to maintain those businesses. In an emergency, such as the inevitable earthquake in Vancouver or other acts of nature, we desperately need local sources of food! The current pandemic has shown us in real time how fragile the food systems and food security can be.

3: Eat Probiotically

Eating probiotically is a choice in diet and lifestyle, whereby we constantly choose to accompany our meals with probiotic and prebiotic foods to feed our microbiome, first and foremost. This is the way of the future.

We, as a culture, need to take control of our own health, starting at the most basic level—*through every single purchase and at every single meal.* We could take reams of supplements (that is, continue to take pills), but it is much more economical, more engaging, and even fun to make these foods ourselves. And it's really quite easy!

The probiotic movement is part of the bottom line of this book—namely, to teach parents, students, teachers, families, and the general population about the background and reasons for embracing a more probiotic lifestyle.

Building a balanced gut microbiome through eating the good bugs and feeding them properly by increasing our intake of fiber is exactly what we need to do as a species, at this time. Feeding our microbiome will improve our individual physical health. Healing our leaky guts *alone* will help us reduce our chronic and rampant cultural inflammation, which appears to be the root of many and perhaps all disease. We can do this, one person at a time.

Through feeding our microbiome and just being aware of the gut-brain connection, we will improve our mental, emotional, and physical health. Making improved food choices and incorporating a daily practice of meditation or self-hypnosis is the way of the future, in terms of maintaining an ability to relax and decompress in our stressed-out society. Learning to relax will *alone* reduce the reliance on the medical health care system immensely.

The daily practice of feeding our microbiome can help ease the strain on our overall healthcare system through more of us taking positive health steps into our own hands. And, even bigger than that, feeding the soil microbiome refusing GMOs, buying organic / biodynamic can help support our planet's recover from the soil up - into the atmosphere, literally.

The food-mood connection in this chapter lies in changing consumer habits—how and where we buy, how we support local producers, and "voting with our food dollars." Consumers are the most powerful tool in making change as we purchase things that conform to our values. Those suppliers or producers we support then have the financial power to continue. As individuals, how we make choices causes a ripple effect that is, quite literally, felt all over the world. The cup of coffee or shirt that you buy and the food you choose (which is shipped from South America or Australia in the off-season, whether you support fair trade, organic, or bio-dynamic) makes a difference to your health and contributes to the health of the planet at the same time. Not only will you be healthier, but you can feel good knowing that your choices improve lives all the way up and down the food chain.

Chapter 9—Key Highlights:

1. Small changes in our shopping, eating, growing, cooking, and cleaning habits can have a huge effect of supporting and cultivating microbial life.

2. We can easily visualize how to nurture our microbiome through this model and change from "the bottom up."

Chapter 10: Harnessing the Power of Our Gut-Brain Connection

The Food-Mood Connection: A Holistic Approach to Understanding the Gut-Brain-Microbiome Relationship has been primarily about the origins and continuing the re-creation and sustainability of the many levels of our microbiome. Of course, it particularly highlights the human gut microbiome. We have followed evolution from the beginning of life on Earth and have seen how there is no separation of all of this life. It is a stark fact of reality that all life is interconnected—even though it has been possible to ignore and even deny it, thus far, simply because our guts are not visible to the naked eye. We have to examine our overall health and look for the myriad symptoms that appear so disconnected to normal people, but are really not.

Just as distant stars and planets are not visible but real, so are the lifeforms found in our microbiomes. Now, we can grasp as to why they are so important. Everything is connected and all creatures create systems. Once one is removed or weakened, the entire system is weakened or removed. This is obvious when we refer to something that all of us are aware, such as the flower and bee system, for example.

Many of us do not think we need to pay attention to what we cannot see. The details of which we are unaware don't seem to matter—until they *do*, as we have seen with the COVID-19 pandemic crisis. In our grandparents' day, there were no big decisions about which foods to choose; they ate what was available, in season. Or they grew it. Nowadays, no matter where someone lives in the world, one can find the food that we crave. It matters not whether it is strawberries in deep winter or the McDonald's burger and fries from home that you want to eat when in Russia or San Francisco—that same exact meal is readily available nearly everywhere.

Oftentimes, we are blissfully unaware of the details of how our bodies function, or don't function, until symptoms demand our critical attention. In fact, this is often the case when our attention is called to the problem that maybe prompted you to read this book. Many of us drift or "sleepwalk" through life, until something happens; until you can no longer just float and drift. You must then take action. That is what happened in my life and it may be why you are reading this as well.

Just as so many diseases are now known to spring from the imbalance of our microbial relationships, so many reasons for curiosity and remedies have abounded. Many of us struggle with anxiety, which is often the first reaction of our bodies signalling for change and relief—the canary in the coal mine, so to speak.

The good news is that all of this can change, with awareness and a few simple guidelines. Often, a shift in our eating habits results from a shift in our thinking and our shopping. As a result, our eating habits evolve. When we know better, we do better. That is what this part of the book is about.

Before I get into some "frequently asked questions," I thought it would be appropriate to share some of my clients' experiences, because they clearly portray how this all works and how "harnessing the power of the gut-brain connection" can really change lives.

So many people have gut issues and they really have no idea that they do!

Client #1: "Anna"

The first client is Anna (a pseudonym). She came to me with several problems—some physical, some mental, and some emotional.

Anna is a young career professional who is married and has a young daughter (two years old). Anna is the breadwinner in the family. She found herself increasingly frustrated with her marriage and her husband, who was underemployed and ended up at home, being responsible for most of the childcare and housework. I suspect he didn't like that very much, as she complained about his addicted abuse of recreational drugs.

Anna is very hardworking, well-educated, and accomplished, although her career seemed stalled and she longed for higher income, more choices in her life, and a better relationship.

Through our interviews, I learned she had some long-term skin issues (acne) and she has some gut/autoimmune issues (Hashimoto's disease) as well. Also, her family history, as a young immigrant with Asian parents, included that she had strained relationships, with both parents, but mostly with her father. She also had a very strained relationship with her mother-in-law. Her gender role was being challenged in her marriage, she was unhappy, and she didn't know how to communicate well with her mother-in-law.

Through hypnosis, we were able to identify key events in her life with her parents that held her back in her work and her in-law relationship. Through that experience, Anna had some intense, heart-to-heart discussions with her husband and her mother-in-law. Her newfound confidence majorly contributed to the positive changes in those relationships. Her husband quit smoking through his own hypnotherapy. Now, their marriage is much less bumpy. They are working together on their own home-based business, they moved houses, and are closer to nature. All of these things are better for the wellbeing of the entire family.

We adjusted her diet to include more fresh foods with probiotic and fermented foods, and she was tested for SIBO (Small Intestine Bacterial Overgrowth), which I suspected she might have.

It was discovered that she actually had SIBO. Her SIBO cleared up since she made these changes. I am not sure how her Hashimoto's sits at the time of this writing, but if she continues on in this way, it has likely improved or will improve.

Client #2: "Penny"

Penny is a lovely, young high school student who suffers from anorexia and Obsessive Compulsive Disorder (OCD). Her parents were literally at their wit's end, after seeing many practitioners, counsellors, and nutrition experts. Their path had taken them from the time Penny was 12 years old to her current age of 16. Then, they came to me. When we met, Penny had been hospitalized and was under a doctor's care and on a strict food-plan.

Penny had several "rituals" she had to do during the course of her day. For example, she had a series of movements and activities she must do before going downstairs to the kitchen in the morning: flicking the light switches, counting stairs, washing her hands in a certain way, and all sorts of things that grew to exhaust her in their growing complexity. She also spoke of being harassed by a "devil voice," who spoke to her almost constantly, telling her to not eat things, telling her she was ugly, and much, much more. Her ruminating thoughts were dragging her down and her deterioration grew worse.

Penny's family eats quite well. They eat healthy, balanced meals. Penny would eat, but in tiny amounts, because she always felt guilty to eat. Even though she had been improving gradually, her "devil voice" haunted her non-stop and she suffered with punishment after forcing herself to increase her intake.

From the current research, we worked on restoring her microbiome by having her take supplements with fiber. We started working on her subconscious mind (SCM) and began filling her SCM with repetitive positive affirmations that were based on what she wants instead of what she doesn't want. We introduced a thrice-daily meditative self-hypnosis that supports her improving mindset, reduces stress, and gave her hope for improvement.

Slowly, Penny's anxiety, inner judge, and negative thinking began to subside and a happy young woman began to emerge. Feedback from her mother the other day was "Penny said today, 'I feel like I don't have an eating disorder anymore.'"

Clearly, changing the mindset with the support of the "second brain" makes fast, permanent change possible!

Moving Forward

This next section is where we bring all of this together, using our minds to control our thoughts and to feed our microbiome well. When we concentrate on feeding our microbiome what it needs, often the result is a reduction of cravings and the creation of the good hormones we need, such as serotonin. When we eat a balanced diet, we repair Leaky Gut Syndrome (LGS).

We need to go back to the old ways when we ate lots of material (fiber and collagen to feed and protect the mucosal gut lining) with thick and rich high-cartilage bone broth.

On top of that, we need to add lots of cruciferous and other vegetables (five to seven per day) for the wide variety of prebiotic fiber to feed the wide complimentary population of microbes.

The last element that is so very important is the element of fermented foods.

Recommendations are that we really ought to eat like our great grandparents did—with a fermented food at every meal. Perhaps we can have fermented milk with our breakfast, pickles with our sandwich at lunch, and fermented vegetables with our main course at dinner.

Homemade products are always much less expensive and because we know the ingredients used, we can feel safe and proud of our products. When we make our own foodstuffs, we can pick our favorite ingredients for freshness, taste, local suppliers, packaging, or reduce salt, sugar and add flavourings and toppings of choice.

Frequently Asked Questions

Lately, when speaking with friends, colleagues, and clients about the material outlined in this book, I learned that some are actually quite familiar with the concept of the microbiome. Over the last ten years, it has become very common in the popular press. The terms "microbiome," "prebiotics," and "probiotics" are even on labels for food and drinks, nowadays. This was unheard of, when I first started doing my research.

When someone is exposed to the gut-brain-microbiome connection in a comprehensive presentation, the confusion can be somewhere in the area of "So, what do I do now?" There are lots of books, videos, and articles out there to choose from, including popular press, peer-reviewed papers, and author-generated books. For more reading suggestions, see the extensive list at the end of this book.

Here are some of the questions people frequently ask me:

1. Because everything is connected, as you show in the Human Ecology diagram, it seems so overwhelming, so how and where do I start?

Overwhelm is something that we all deal with. The more I learn, the more I know there is to learn.

The most important thing is do remember the Serenity Prayer: "God grant me the serenity to accept the things I cannot change, the courage to change the things I can, and the wisdom to know the difference." Do what you can. Start with yourself. Work from the inside out. Put on your oxygen mask first, before helping anyone else. All of this sounds a bit trite, but it really is true.

What I have done over the years is to be aware of what I am eating. I buy organic foods, as much as possible. I eat fermented foods with almost every meal. I eat the high-fiber all-stars: cruciferous vegetables, asparagus, onions, shallots, and garlic. I eat fish, two or three times a week. I take all the supplements that my ND (naturopathic doctor) tells me to. I will admit that I have been lax on my exercise because I have been working really hard the last few years, but I have committed to biking and walking more and getting out in nature more often. Living in Vancouver, we are blessed by being surrounded by nature all around us. Fresh air, water, and green plants abound!

2. I'm sure everyone is different but what is the prescription for someone wanting to heal their gut? I don't think there is a way to measure how leaky it is, for starters, but does a strict protocol of probiotics and fermented foods every day, plus the intake of fiber do it?

I am not a doctor nor have I ever discussed or known about a limited timeline or a prescription that lasts for a limited time. As far as I am concerned, this is a lifestyle; a lifelong commitment. For those of us who have had difficulties with Leaky Gut Syndrome, LGS is probably something we are susceptible to, and might need to monitor and maintain for life.

Feeding our microbiome instead of eating "what we like" is a fairly bold change for many of us, but it seems to be essential to modern life, if we are to get our health back. And we *can*.

3. What is the timeframe for repair? Is it a month? Six months? Then, what do I do? Maintain it or what?

This may be the million-dollar question! I don't know. After saying what I did in the last response, I really have no idea. I suppose in the "real world," if we solved all the water, soil, and air issues and had only organic food and no pollution, etc., we could be lax about our attitude towards foods we buy or grow and eat.

I am very hopeful during this time of the Big Pause (the COVID-19 pandemic) that we come out the other side acknowledging all the good that we can glean from this time of slowing down, not driving, flying, or buying so much. If we can recreate our food system in a way that is similar to what it was 100 years, ago, we have a chance. It will likely take all of us assuming much more responsibility for our own health—and maybe even growing our own food.

4. Is it okay to take my probiotic pills in the morning?

Many of my clients and friends tell me that they take their pills in the morning with their coffee of tea. This is not the ideal time. Often, people do not eat in the morning—and the probiotics (your "good" bacteria and yeasts) need to be fed! As well, people often rely too much on pills and supplements.

I was always taught in university that it is much better to get our nutrients from food and not from pills. This is before we knew that most of our food wasn't the same as was grown 100 years ago; an apple is not always the apple you think it is. However, when taking probiotic supplements, it is most important to ensure that the microbial life forms get their food while you get yours. So, when taking supplements, eat them with fibrous foods, as suggested and discussed in the previous chapters. If the probiotics are not fed, they will die off and be eliminated. Feed them first.

5. You have written that immunity, obesity, and mental health begin with the microbiome. How can they all be related, when they seem so drastically different?

This is one of the fascinating things about studying this "organ" and the communication back and forth between our brain and our "second brain." All are connected and it is just not intuitive, since we have developed such a disconnection between all our systems in the Western medical models. We have specialists in all parts of the body and the discovery of the microbiome has started to bring all of these medical specialists back together to find a common footing.

Immunity has been a primary focus since the COVID-19 pandemic began, and I feel quite confident that research will elicit evidence that an unhealthy microbiome plays a huge role in our defense against viruses such as this. There has already been evidence in cases where individuals with "pre-existing conditions" in the USA, particularly with Diabetes and obesity, were among the most prevalent in the hospitalized COVID-19 cases as well as in the deaths reported. Both of those conditions are definitely related to dysbiosis and a dysfunctional gut—a leaky gut, in particular.

Mental health is especially connected to a leaky gut and dysbiosis. This was proven again and again, in everything from ADD/ADHD, MS, Parkinson's, Alzheimer's, bi-polar disorder, anxiety, depression, OCD, anorexia, etc. There was a story on the news the other night where a young female medical doctor in New York City (who was very successful, accomplished, well-loved, and more) came down with the COVID-19 virus. She got amazingly ill, but did recover, albeit not completely. She came back work early, had a breakdown, and actually committed suicide. This was after having no apparent mental health issues up to that point. As a result, it is now speculated that mental health is hugely affected by the virus—which would make sense, if our immunity and our mental health are all precipitated from our gut health. So interesting!

We shall see where this new material takes science and us in the coming days, weeks, months, and years, as our society patches together a new life after this crisis. I welcome the challenge and invite you all to join me in feeding and caring for all the biomes and microbiomes on Earth, from the top of our heads to the bottom of our toes and beyond!

Aside from the questions I mentioned, I am sure you have more questions. I would be happy to help you answer them. All you have to do is reach out to me!

In this chapter, the food-mood connection is clear. When we support our microbiome as well as take control of our thoughts, we can change our physical, mental, and emotional health. Taking specific measures with particular foods can support gut health, reduce Leaky Gut Syndrome, and produce more hormones and other chemicals that enable cellular and system health. All of this can help prevent, maintain, and develop better immunity, mental health, and control of our weight. Of particular importance is the fact that our SCM is connected to our microbiome, and impacts our behaviors and habits. Our subconscious acts or paradigms must be changed if we expect to get different results in our day-to-day lives. Hypnotherapy is a great tool for enacting such improved changes, as we have seen with my clients, Anna and Penny. (To learn more about this tool OR ask me your questions, contact me via www.Pivotal-Hypnotherapy.com or go to www.calendly.com/lynnepotterlord/ to book a free 20-minute telephone or Zoom consultation.)

Chapter 10—Key Highlights:

1. Client experience enhances the power of the physical, mental and emotional health improvement process. Making diet adjustments, raising awareness of how life is approached and how small changes of subconscious thought processes can have huge impacts on our mental and emotional health. This process is how Hypno-Life Coaching can support amazing life changes.

2. Small, practical changes in our day-to-day lives can make an enormous difference, from the microbial level to the entire ecosystem.

3. Remember to feed your probiotics so they don't die off!

Chapter 11: Specific Food Information (+ Recipes!)

The purpose of this section is to outline some of the things we can do in our day-to-day lives to increase the positive microbial culture in our bodies. This is done through eating probiotic foods and also eating prebiotic foods to feed the microbes. Foundational to this is to heal our leaky gut so we can decrease inflammation at the source. To do this, we can increase our intake of fermented foods by eating some at every meal (or most meals) and increase the amount of fiber present in every meal. By increasing a little bit of each during every meal, we won't need to add huge portions of these foods in one meal. Thus, we can minimally tweak our habits.

For example, I add vegetables to everything I cook, even eggs and omelets, smoothies, and juices, and definitely to soups and sauces. I eat fermented condiments such as mustard, ketchup, pesto, and mayonnaise. I add a spoon of pickled vegetables, kimchi, or sauerkraut to the side of my plate with breakfast, lunch, and dinner. I add kefir to my morning oatmeal. I include pickled cabbage on my plate with my eggs. I will put kefir or yogurt sauce on baked or mashed potatoes. Over time, all of this adds up to an increase in good bacteria in my body.

Truth be told, not all of these probiotic foods I eat will survive the stomach acid. I find that what I eat and drink can either be diminished through the stomach or it sometimes suffers abuse later in the process, by my behaviors. Periods of high stress or bouts of drinking more alcohol over Christmas, for example, can affect the diversity and volume of a good, balanced bacterial environment. When I travel, I carry specific probiotics with me (which do not require refrigeration). Because local water treatments and varying climates can affect the strains of probiotics in the environment, I make sure I bring my own.

This book is intended to support the idea of good foods, portable and useful for lunches as well as being healthy, probiotic or gut supportive, and easy to eat with one's hands. "Hand-held" or "finger food" are descriptors that comes to mind. Considering the agreement reached with school counsellors over the food and anxiety connection (all backed up by science), it is clearly essential, particularly for students in school, to eat a solid healthy lunch—different from many of the ones we currently see.[109]

A few labelled containers for seeds, crackers, eggs, cheese, or fish, and a thermos or insulated water bottle for broth or kefir, as well as some fresh or pickled vegetables and fresh fruit is all that it takes to make a meal healthier. Even though it takes a small amount of effort to put this together, the benefits are staggering.

Probiotic Foods as a Foundation for a Healthy Gut: Bone Broth

The most basic and important food that enables a healthy gut is collagen-laden, homemade bone broth. Our grandmothers were right: chicken soup will heal just about everything! The collagen from the cartilage in or on the bones dissolves during the long, slow simmer. Calcium enriches the broth through adding acetic acid (either lemon juice or a vinegar of your choice), which leaches out minerals and eventually dissolves the bones, yielding a healing broth that will give a rich and strong gut lining.

Something that we have lost touch with in modern times, through the refrigeration and processing of foods, is the habit of saving bones for times of famine. There is evidence of cave-dwellers wrapping bones in skins and storing them in deep, cool pits for later, when fresh food was more intermittent or scarce. Much nutrition can be leached out of bones, and many cultures and their cuisine evolved and revolved around a stock pot on the back of the stove, harvesting any and all scraps, boiling bad germs out of them, and getting nutrition from whatever was available. Before refrigeration, this was actually essential.

Using Basic Bone Broth

One of the best ways to heal a leaky gut is by repairing the mucosal lining of your intestines (which protects the cells of the gut lining), allowing cells to heal and backfill spaces or leaks. The easiest and least expensive way to support this process is to create homemade bone broth, using bones from an organic cooked chicken or turkey carcass. You can also cook the chicken whole and use the cooked meat for other meals, if desired.

Of course, other bones can be used, such as beef, pork, lamb, or fish. Those bones would always be organic or wild, since toxins concentrate the higher on the food chain the animal is, and mammals are the highest. With humans and pigs being omnivorous, it is essential to avoid such toxins because they get stored in the body and need assistance to be removed.

Homemade stock is always preferable to commercially processed stock (unless they are locally made, small batch products with free-range, organic chicken bones). These types of small batch products (markets and farmers) are usually made in the homemade style and not flavoured with artificial bouillon powders or the like.

Bone broth can be used during fasting or intermittent fasting.[110]

Bone broth is also a great way to fast-track healing, twofold. First, by not having solid food to process, your gut gets a rest as well as a cleanse. Second, by supplying collagen to the system in the broth, the microbiome utilizes the collagen to replenish the mucosal lining and seals leaky gut junctions at the cellular level.

When cooking real bones, the cartilage (collagen) is dissolved in the stock as the bones are cooked, which is enhanced by adding apple cider vinegar (or other types of vinegar) to the broth and simmering it for 12-24 hours. As described in the section about leaky guts, it is essential to promote a healed mucosal lining of the gut.

A widely diverse community of probiotic species also contributes to the diversity of species that contributes to the protection of the gut lining. Adding vinegar to the stock increases the calcium content and breaks down the cartilage in the stock. For people not consuming dairy, this is a great source of dairy-free calcium. When we add a variety of vegetables to the broth, this then becomes an extremely concentrated source of prebiotic nutrients to feed the microbiome. Varying the types of vegetables adds to the diversity of microbial species that can be supported and maintained in our resident and transient species.

• Recipe #1: Chicken Bone Broth (Using Organic, Bio-dynamic, or Non-medicated Chickens)

Ingredients:

Collection of organic bones
1 whole 5-lb. (2 kg) chicken, cut in pieces
5 quarts (4-5 L) water
3 bay leaves
2 stems of celery hearts
2 carrots, peeled and roughly chopped
1 large onion, chopped
½ bunch flat-leafed parsley
1 tsp (5 mL) whole black peppercorns
2 tsp (10 mL) sea salt
½ tsp (2½ mL) dried oregano
3-5 sprigs fresh thyme
1-2 tsp (5-10 mL) balsamic or apple cider vinegar
5 garlic cloves, smashed

Method:

1. In a large stock pot, combine all ingredients and bring to a boil.
2. Reduce heat and simmer for 45 minutes, until the meat is cooked. Meat can be removed when cooked and stored for another purpose.
3. Remove chicken pieces, then cool.
4. Take meat of the bones.
5. Shred or chop meat into small pieces and freeze or refrigerate for future use.
6. Return the bones to stock, add vinegar, and continue simmer on low for 12-24 hours.
7. Remove the bones and strain the rest of the ingredients or blend into stock.
8. Cool, then divide the stock into portions and can or freeze.

● Chapter Recipe #2: Fish Bone Broth

(This recipe has been modified from Dr. Mercola's cookbook called *Ketofast: Rejuvenate Your Health with a Step-by-Step Guide to Timing Your Ketogenic Meals.*)

Ingredients (3-4L):

2 T (30 mL) coconut oil
2 celery stalks, chopped
2 onions, chopped
1 carrot, chopped
½ cup (120 mL) white wine (optional)
3-4 whole fish bone carcasses, including heads (such as snapper, salmon, or other)
3 T (45 mL) apple cider vinegar
4 quarts (3-4 L) water
Handful of thyme and parsley sprigs

Method:

1. Melt the oil and sauté the vegetables for 3-6 minutes or until soft.
2. Pour in the wine.
3. Add fish carcasses and cover with cold water.
4. Add vinegar and bring to boil.
5. Skim off the scum and impurities, as they rise to the top.
6. Tie the herbs and add them to the pot.
7. Reduce heat and simmer for at least 3 hours.
8. Remove the carcasses and strain the liquid through a sieve into a large storage container.
9. Cool overnight and remove the fat layer. Broth should be thick and gelatinous, depending on the time bones were cooked.
10. Transfer to smaller containers and use as desired.

• Recipe #3: Spiced Squash Soup (Serves 4)

(This recipe has been modified from Dr. Mercola's cookbook called *Ketofast: Rejuvenate Your Health with a Step-by-Step Guide to Timing Your Ketogenic Meals.*)

Ingredients:

3 T (45 mL) coconut oil or good quality animal fat
1 large butternut squash peeled, seeded & diced
1 carrot, diced
1 large onion, diced
4 cloves garlic, crushed
1-1½ quarts (1-1½ L) chicken bone broth (or other broth)
2 T (30 mL) finely grated ginger
1½ tsp (7½mL) ground cumin
6 saffron threads
1 tsp (5 mL) chili flakes
1 cup (250 mL) coconut cream
Sea salt and ground black pepper
Cilantro and mint leaves, for garnish
Chili powder, to serve
2 T (30 mL) Ras el Hanout

Ras el Hanout is a Moroccan exotic, earthy mix made from just eight spices:
- 1 tsp (5 mL) ground cumin
- 1 tsp (5 mL) ground ginger
- 1 tsp (5 mL) salt
- 1 tsp (5 mL) freshly ground black pepper
- ½ tsp (2½ mL) ground cinnamon
- ½ tsp (2½ mL) ground coriander seeds
- ½ tsp (2½ mL) cayenne
- ½ tsp (2½ mL) allspice
- ½ tsp (2½ mL) ground cloves

Method:

1. Heat the oil and fry the squash in a large saucepan over medium heat.
2. Add carrot, onion, and garlic.
3. Stir occasionally for about 10 minutes, until the onion is transparent.

4. Add broth, ginger, and spices (if using).
5. Reduce heat and simmer for 30 minutes until vegetables are tender, stirring occasionally.
6. Add coconut cream and puree the soup with a handheld blender.
7. Season to taste with salt and pepper.
8. Ladle soup into bowls.
9. Drizzle with coconut cream, yogurt, or kefir and serve with cilantro, mint leaves, and chili powder.

• Going Gluten-Free

Eating gluten-free is not the easiest thing in the world to do, especially in a safe way. Gluten is in almost everything, so it is really difficult to avoid. We can eliminate bread from a diet by just stopping eating it. However, this can be difficult for many of us and especially challenging when packing a lunch kit. A sandwich for lunch is a classic and easy meal to prepare; we can include all the food groups and eat it easily with our hands.

If we have gluten sensitivities or recognize it would be prudent to reduce gluten in our diets or remove it completely, we search out good substitutes. Unfortunately, most gluten-free products use rice as a substitute. Higher rates of eating rice, especially brown rice, can increase health issues with the natural increase in arsenic, for example.

Finding that perfect thing to use as a bread substitute can be both for function, meaning to hold things on them as well as eat them as finger foods. For example, celery and carrot sticks or other vegetables are often used to scoop humus, cottage cheese, salsas, smoked salmon, tuna salad, or other toppings. Rounds of cucumber or zucchini are great when hollowed out a bit and filled with appetizer options, such as cream cheese mixtures, fruit and cottage cheese blends, or fish toppings. Another substitute that is growing in popularity is lettuce wraps. These are great for holding scoops of mixtures as well, and can hold more than just a dipping function. Lettuce wraps can be used when making tacos (with any meat, fish, or bean filling) or other wrapped sandwiches. Additions can be stir-fried vegetables, noodle mixtures, seeds, or grain mixtures with quinoa.

One of my favorites is seed crackers. I discovered those crackers a few years ago and have made them often. Easy to use in a variety of ways, they can be served as chips, if they are broken into small pieces, or bread, if you cut them into larger chunks. They keep well for several weeks in a tin or Tupperware container stored in a cool, dry place.

• Recipe #4: Anna's Flat Seed Crackers

This recipe was given to me when visiting Anna, a lovely Swedish woman I met in France. They are delicious, gluten-free, grain-free, and can be a bread or cracker substitute when packing lunches. They also contain Omega-3 oils, which can be enhanced by grinding the flax seeds.

Serve with dips, hummus, cheese, olives, avocado, or tapenade. Smaller chunks can be used as chips for dips. Seeds at the bottom of the container can be saved for salad toppings.

Ingredients:

1½ cups (355 mL) mix of flax and/or chia seeds
½ cup (120 mL) sesame seeds
½ cup (120 mL) sunflower seeds
½ cup (120 mL) pumpkin seeds
2 T (60 mL) olive oil
1 cup (250 mL) boiling water (or more)
½ tsp (2½ mL) salt
½ cup (120 mL) cornstarch

Method:

Choice of seasonings can be very creative, choosing from black pepper, chili, turmeric, onion or garlic powder, oregano, rosemary, or thyme. Even slightly ground sea salt sprinkled on top before baking is tasty. If desired, small chopped pieces of dried fruit can be added for a more "cookie-like" approach, in which case cinnamon might be added instead of the savory spices. Recipe can be easily doubled.

1. Preheat oven to 375F. In a large bowl, mix all ingredients together.
2. Allow about 10 minutes for the chia or flax seeds to soften and gelatinize.
3. Line a baking sheet with parchment paper and spray with oil. Add more water as necessary as the mixture will stiffen while sitting between baking batches.
4. Spread the mixture out on the baking sheet until thin and flat (<1 ml).
5. Bake for 30 -40 minutes, or more depending on thickness. Check so as not to burn the edges. Turn 1⁄2 way through baking process.
6. Remove from oven and slice into cracker shapes. Pizza wheel works well.
7. Carefully turn the crackers over and bake for another 20-30 minutes.
8. Allow to cool.
9. Store in airtight container for a week or two.

● **Recipe #5: Spicy Pumpkin Seed Snacks**

Ingredients:

1 cup (250 mL) raw pumpkin seeds (or a mix of other seeds)
1 tsp (5 mL) chili powder
¼ tsp (1 mL) cayenne powder (2 mL makes it *spicy*)
1 tsp (5 mL) coarse sea salt
2 tsp (10 mL) lime juice
Optional spices: eliminate chili powder and add turmeric, mustard, garlic, dill, or whatever you or the children prefer.

Method:

1. Preheat oven to 350°F.
2. Line a rimmed baking sheet with parchment paper.
3. In a medium bowl, mix seeds, salt, and cayenne.
4. Add lime juice and stir until seeds are coated.
5. Turn the seeds onto parchment paper and spread them out in a single layer. Be sure to scrape all spices onto seeds from bowl.
6. Bake for 10 minutes.
7. Cool, divide into portions, and enjoy, topped with hummus, other spreads, nut-butters, or cheeses.

This recipe can easily be doubled.

● Recipe #6: Beet Hummus

Hummus is a great food for snacks and lunches. It is a protein (chickpeas) and provides fiber to feed the microbiome. It is filling and works well with vegetable sticks. It is easy to pack and easy to eat. The beets add color and an interesting taste.

Ingredients:

4 medium-sized beets
2 T (30 mL) tahini sesame seed paste
⅓ cup (80 mL) canned peeled chickpeas
3 T (75 mL) lemon juice
1 small clove garlic, chopped
1 T (15 mL) ground cumin
1 T (15 mL) lemon zest (from approximately 2 lemons)
Generous pinch of sea salt or kosher salt
Fresh ground pepper, to taste

Method:

1. Cut off the tops of the beets and scrub the roots clean.
2. Cover beets with water in a saucepan and simmer until tender, about 20 minutes.
3. Cool and then peel.
4. Blend all ingredients in a food processor until your desired consistency is reached.

● Recipe #7: Lemon Artichoke Hummus

Ingredients:

1 cup (250 mL) artichoke heart (canned, rinsed, dried & chopped)
¼ cup (60 mL) lemon juice (from 2 lemons)
¼ cup (60 mL) water
1/3 cup (80 mL) tahini, stirred well
2 T (30 mL) olive oil (plus extra for drizzling)
1 cup (250 mL) chickpeas, drained and rinsed
1 clove garlic, minced
½ tsp (2½ mL) salt
½ tsp (2½ mL) lemon zest
½ tsp (2½ mL) cayenne pepper, divided
2 tsp (10 mL) fresh parsley

Method:

1. Blend (or food process) the chickpeas and liquids until smooth.
2. Add other ingredients and blend again until smooth.
3. Add artichoke hearts and blend on "pulse" to the desired consistency, leaving some chunks.
4. Garnish with some chunky pieces and a sprinkle of cayenne or paprika.
5. Serve hot or cold with vegetable sticks, seed crackers, toast, or pita chips.

• Recipe #8: All-Dressed Kale Chips

Ingredients:

2 bunches green kale (or other sturdy greens)
1 T (15 mL) olive oil
1½ tsp (7½ mL) apple cider vinegar
1 tsp (5 mL) garlic powder
1 tsp (5 mL) chili powder
½ tsp (2½ mL) onion powder
½ tsp (2½ mL) smoked paprika
½ tsp (2½ mL) fine grain or pink Himalayan sea salt
¼ tsp (1-2 mL) cayenne pepper (optional)

Method:

1. Preheat oven to 350°F.
2. Line a large rimmed baking sheet with parchment paper.
3. Remove the leaves from the stems of the kale and roughly tear it up into large pieces. Compost the stems (or freeze for smoothies).
4. Wash and spin the leaves until thoroughly dry.
5. Put the kale leaves into a large bowl. Massage in the oil until all the nooks and crannies are coated in oil.
6. Sprinkle on the spices or seasonings, then toss to combine.
7. Spread out the kale onto prepared baking sheet in a single layer, being sure not to overcrowd the kale.
8. Bake for 10 minutes, rotate the pan, and bake 12-15 minutes more, until the kale begins to firm up and crisp. The kale will look shrunken, but this is normal. (Bake for 25 minutes, in total.)

• Fermented Foods

Basic recipes to start on this probiotic path to *The Food-Mood Connection: A Holistic Approach to Understanding the Gut-Brain-Microbiome Relationship* are the fermented trilogy included here. These are fermented dairy products, fermented tea, and fermented or "pickled vegetables." The intent herein is to share ideas of how to create take-along lunches that are easy, very healthy, and even fun to make and eat. The great thing about making some of these fermenters is that they become a living science experiment on the kitchen counter. Children love watching them grow, develop, bubble, and squeak. Fermented foods create interest, intrigue, and conversation around the process that can be watched through the glass jar. The best thing is that we can create the missing puzzle pieces to health that can be easily incorporated into our lunches taken to work and school each day.

Since the beginning of man (and as discussed, especially before modern refrigeration), fresh foods were harvested, and some needed to be eaten that day or the next. The freshness of the foods could be extended by a variety of means, including chilling, freezing, salting, smoking, dehydrating, sweetening, fermentation, and canning. Some anthropologists even speculate that agriculture itself was developed 10,000 years ago to grow wheat—not to necessarily eat; that was a by-product. The theory is that wheat was grown originally to brew beer! Grapes were grown primarily to make wine. Creating drinks with grains and fruit became a normal way to preserve the nutritional values of the foods. Learning to bottle them made them easy to transport with the army and navy.

At that time in history, obtaining clean water was difficult to find or transport to the people. Having beer and wine to drink, good bacteria kept the product from going "bad." Plus, the addition of a little feel-good as a by-product made alcohol one of the original fermented foods we co-evolved with.

Fermented foods have been with us since the dawn of time. Because fresh foods cannot remain fresh indefinitely, before refrigeration, humans had to take advantage of a variety of ways to preserve food. Some were seasonal. In the winter, we used freezing and root cellars to keep foods cold. In the summer, we dehydrated foods in the sun and wind. We added sugar. We added salt. We juiced and stewed fruits and vegetables and then, when we didn't eat it all, it started to spoil. That's how we invented beer, wine, and compotes.

Grain goes rancid and molds. Milk spoils. Fruit bruises and rots. When our ancestors cooked them, apples lasted longer because they were cooked, and the bad bugs were killed off. The easiest way to kill bugs is by high temperature. Cooking decreases bacteria for a while. This is the "soup on the stove" concept.

Before refrigeration, a wide variety of fermented foods became commonplace when humans began practicing agriculture. Yogurt and kefir are such foods. We didn't kill all of the animals; we kept some for foods. We kept chickens for eggs. We kept cows and goats for milk. Milk, however, doesn't last in a fresh form for long. When we leave milk sitting on the counter, it takes very little time for it to turn to kefir, yogurt, or cheese. All it needs to speed up the process is a little inoculation of a starter culture.

Fermented Dairy Products

Some of the most common fermented foods in the world are fermented dairy products. The most popular are yogurts, kefirs, and cheeses. All of these products are made using cow's milk, although they can be made using other milks such as goat, coconut, almond, or soya milk.

The basic process of fermentation is totally natural and has occurred (without our encouragement) for millennia. Everything eventually breaks down, and foods are some of the quickest things to "turn" towards fermentation and decomposition.

With domestication and animal husbandry, other food products also developed. At first, it was speculated that they occurred naturally. Humans then began to assist the different organisms. Yeasts inoculated beer, wine, bread, and cheese. Eventually, people noticed that certain things made products taste better and so they added a "starter" culture from a batch they liked. To this day, this practice continues.

Some fermented dairy products have more "good bacteria" than others. For example, regular, commercially-produced yogurt will contain one or two different bacteria. This is due to whatever starter is included in the manufacturing process. Most kefir products, however, are made to contain over 15 different varieties of microbes, bacteria, yeasts, fungi, and protozoa. This can make a huge difference when one is attempting to build a wider variety of organisms in their gut system.

At the time of this writing, research is actually on the brink of discovering the benefits of some of these specific probiotic organisms. Initial research shows that specific needs of the body can sometimes intervene to "heal," by filling a need in a particular chemical cascade in the cells or body at large. This is incredibly exciting, considering all the help we need in our food systems, body systems, and essentially, all other interdependent systems.

● Recipe #9: Plain Yogurt

The first time I explained this yogurt recipe to a friend she replied, "That is so easy! Why doesn't everyone just make their own? It's really very good—and much less expensive." Indeed. Why don't we? Here's how you can:

Ingredients:

1 quart (1L) of whole milk (at any fat level, using any type of milk: cow, goat, almond, coconut, soy, etc.)
¼ cup (60 mL) fresh yogurt as a starter (or dried envelope of a starter culture, to inoculate)
Thermometer

Method:

1. Heat the milk in a saucepan to 180°F. Do not boil. We don't want to kill the starter with too high a temperature.
2. When at temperature, remove from heat at let milk cool to 100°F. To speed it up, place the pot in an ice bath to cool.
3. Place yogurt starter (or 60-80 mL of the last batch) in a sterile jar large enough for the whole amount of milk. Leave about an inch (2½ cm) of headspace at the top of the jar. Cover the jar with the lid and stir vigorously or shake, to combine the starter with the warmed milk.
4. Place the jar in an incubator, an insulated cooler with hot water, or just leave it in a warm spot to ferment for 12-24 hours.
5. Wrap with a towel to insulate and keep the temperature even, especially if it is drafty.
6. It is ready when it thickens. Yogurt can be thickened further by hanging a cheesecloth over a bowl and draining this batch to remove the water.
7. Refrigerate when taste and consistency is to your preference. Move to small portion jars for lunch kits, if preferred.

NOTE: Yogurt is a great sweet snack when mixed with chopped or mashed fresh fruit, berries, seed granola, or added extracts such as vanilla or powdered cinnamon.

Yogurt makes savory dips for eating with vegetables such as carrot, celery, fennel, or jicama sticks. Add dill, curry, or turmeric, onion, or garlic powder or any other herb/spice combination. If you like a thicker yogurt consistency for dips or spreads, you can strain this (through a cheesecloth over a colander in a large bowl) to remove more liquid.

• Milk Kefir

Kefir is another popular and very beneficial fermented milk product. This product is more a drinkable product and is great plain or for mixing with flavoured spices or fruit. Easily packable for lunch, it is also full of good probiotics—there are about 10 times more microbial varieties in it than yogurt. (It is possible to make kefir using commercial product as a starter, using the method in the yogurt recipe, if the kefir grains are difficult to locate.)

Benefits of drinking kefir:

- Loaded with valuable enzymes, easily digestible complete proteins, vitamins, and minerals
- Supplies your body with billions of healthy bacteria and yeast strains
- Helps manage free radicals in the body
- Complete protein that is high in minerals and vitamins, especially the B vitamins
- Helps to establish healthy bowel flora
- Helps to prevent the growth of harmful bacteria in the body and reduces incidence of colitis

• Recipe #10: Milk Kefir

Ingredients:

2 cups (500 mL) fresh milk (any variety can be used, similar to yogurt)
2 T (30 mL) of kefir grains
A 2-quart (2L) or ½-gallon mason jar

Method:

1. Place 1-2 T (15-30mL) of kefir grains in a clean glass jar. A two-quart or ½-gallon mason jar works well. Add 2 cups (500 mL) fresh milk. Any type of milk will work, including cow, goat, and coconut. The milk may be room temperature or chilled. You may want to allow an extra hour for fermentation, if you are using cold milk.
2. Gently stir the contents, cover the jar with a cloth or a lid left slightly ajar, and move to a location away from direct sunlight. This might be a cupboard, pantry, or darker side of the kitchen.
3. Allow the mixture to ferment for a minimum of 24 hours. It is not advisable to go beyond 48 hours. Pour the contents of the jar into a strainer. Some websites suggest avoiding metal strainers and utensils, while others say it doesn't matter because of the short duration of their contact with the kefir.
4. Take the strained grains, place them in a clean glass jar, and begin the process again. (You can "rest" the grains in the refrigerator covered in milk or yogurt, which must be changed every seven days.) Optional: Leave the strained kefir at room temperature for another 24 hours, to increase its nutritional value. The kefir will become sourer, so feel free to enjoy it after the initial 24-hour period, as it is officially fermented and nutritious at that point.
5. Chill and enjoy.

• Kefir Products

Kefir is a great base for many probiotic products. We can eat or drink kefir products easily with every meal. Kefir can be served chilled and "plain" (unflavoured)—and be quite tasty and enjoyable.

Some of the best ideas that we use in my home are included here.

Savory Kefir Topping or Dips:

Kefir can be mixed with herbs and spices to create a great dip that can easily be taken in a lunch kit to eat with vegetables or fruits. Among my favorites are: garlic (fresh or powdered); curry or turmeric powder; dill (fresh, ground, or crushed seeds); celery seed (crushed); chili sauce; and mustard powder, prepared or seeds (crushed). If a thicker consistency is required for a particular purpose, blend cottage cheese with the mixture to make it more substantial

Sweeter suggestions:

When looking for something a bit sweet, a dollop of mashed fruit or compote can be stirred in.

To add interest and/or anti-inflammatory properties, herbs or spices can be sprinkled on top. Among my favorites are cinnamon (for sweetness) or turmeric and ginger (for a spicy blast).

Ice cream, anyone?

● **Recipe #11: Kefir Ice Cream**

My absolute favorite thing to do with kefir is make ice cream or smoothies in a blender. (I have a heavy-duty Vitamix, but other blenders or food processers can also work.)

Start with:

½-1 cup (120-250 mL) plain kefir (per serving)

Add in:

½-1 cup (120-250 mL per serving) frozen fruit chunks (no sugar added)

I like berry and mango combinations.

Blend until smooth.

Eat with a spoon or drink with a straw, depending on the amount of kefir or servings required. I also sometimes add in extra probiotic powder if I feel like I haven't been getting enough in my diet that week.

● Kombucha

Kombucha is an ancient Japanese probiotic drink made from sweet tea. Made similarly to yogurt and kefir described previously, the basic drink starts with a freshly made product, with a "starter culture" added in, to induce fermentation.

The basic tea is made to specific measurements. The starter is added, along with a small portion of vinegar and a small serving of kombucha tea from a previous batch.

A variety of teas are suitable for making kombucha. However, teas with additional oils and flavourings can sometimes be unsuitable, due to the interference of the oils with the bacteria growth. The large variety of bacteria in kombucha are grown on a layer of accumulated microbial life called a SCOBY, an acronym that stands for "Symbiotic Culture of Bacteria and Yeasts."

• Recipe #12: Kombucha

Equipment:

1 quart-sized to 1 gallon-sized glass jar (1 L to 4L)
Plastic or wooden spoon
Tight-weave cloth
Paper towel
Coffee filter or air lock
Screw-on lid or rubber band (to secure the cover to the jar)

Ingredients:

Active kombucha SCOBY (Symbiotic Culture of Bacteria and Yeasts)
Loose tea or tea bags
White sugar
Filtered water
Starter tea *or* distilled white vinegar (apple cider vinegar and rice vinegar are *not* appropriate for making kombucha tea)

Ingredient Ratios for Making Different Amounts of Kombucha

Container Size	Tea	Sugar	Water	Starter Tea or Vinegar
One quart (1 L)	1-2 tsp (7-10 mL) loose tea *or* 2 tea bags	¼ cup (60 mL)	2-3 cup (500-750 mL)	½ cup (125 mL)
½ Gallon (2 L)	1 T (15 mL) loose tea *or* 4 tea bags	½ cup (120 mL)	1½-1¾ quarts (1½-1¾ L)	1 cup (250 mL)
Gallon (4L)	2 T (30 mL) loose tea *or* 8 tea bags	1 cup (250 mL)	3-3½ quarts (3-3½ L)	2 cups (500 mL)

Before You Begin:

If you have purchased a dehydrated kombucha tea starter culture, activate a dehydrated kombucha SCOBY (Symbiotic Culture of Bacteria and Yeasts) to get started.

NOTE: Using a metal tea ball that contains loose tea for making kombucha is acceptable but the tea ball should be removed before adding the SCOBY and starter tea, so the tea ball will not come into contact with the SCOBY.

Method:

1. Combine the hot water and the sugar in a glass jar. Stir until the sugar dissolves.
2. The water should be hot enough to steep the tea but does not have to be boiling.
3. Place the tea or tea bags in the sugar water to steep.
4. Cool the mixture to 68-85°F. The tea may be left in the liquid as it cools or it may be removed after the first 10-15 minutes. The longer the tea is left in the liquid, the stronger the tea will be.
5. Remove the tea bags or completely strain the loose tea leaves from the liquid.
6. Add the starter tea from a previous batch to the liquid. If you do not have starter tea, distilled white vinegar may be substituted.
7. Add an active kombucha SCOBY.
8. Cover the jar with a tight-weave towel or coffee filter and secure with the screw-on lid or a rubber band.
9. Allow the mixture to sit undisturbed at 68-85°F, out of direct sunlight, for 7-30 days, or to taste. The longer the kombucha ferments, the less sweet and sourer it will taste.
10. Pour kombucha off the top of the jar for consuming. Retain the SCOBY and enough liquid from the bottom of the jar to use as starter tea for the next batch.
11. The finished kombucha can be flavored and bottled, if desired, or enjoyed plain.

Flavoring and Bottling Kombucha

Once the kombucha has finished culturing, remove the SCOBY to use again in a later batch. Keep the resting SCOBY and feed it with fresh sugar water from time to time or it will die.

Chill and enjoy it plain or add flavoring with juice, zest, extracts, or fresh fruit. There is no limit to the flavoring possibilities.

A second fermentation can be made with kombucha after the flavouring. It can be rested again, with a bit more sugar, allowing it to ferment further and increase the bubbles.

• Fermented Vegetables

Fermented vegetables have been essential to our survival as a species and are still part of many cultures around the world. Enabling vegetables to ferment in a controlled environment has allowed them to be harvested at one time of the year and still be edible weeks and months later. Classic examples of this process are the various styles of kimchi from Korean cuisine. Pickled fresh vegetables are done in the same kind of pickling process. Easy and favorite ones are pickled carrots and beets, dill cucumbers, and beans or asparagus.

Kimchi is a traditional Korean fermented vegetable dish that has been longstanding since before the first documented recipe in 1670. Kimchi has almost 200 noted variations. It is a staple in Korea and is growing around the world.

Kimchi would be made in a large crockery jar, wrapped in a cloth or tarp of some kind, and then stored in a "root cellar" or even just buried in the backyard in order to keep the mixture cool and dry. This was an early form of refrigeration, but what it accomplished was to slow down the rate of spoilage or fermentation so the food would last for the winter.

Kimchi was typically made with a cabbage base, often with carrots or other root vegetables, maybe with the addition of a fruit, such as an apple or pear. Sometimes, onion or garlic was added. Chili was also a part of the recipe. People often think they don't like kimchi because manufactured products are often high in chili and difficult for westerners to eat. The chili helps to keep the contaminants down; in that way, it is a preservative.

Kimchi is added to salads and soups. It is eaten at almost every meal in countries like Korea and Vietnam. A basic broth that has sat on the back of the stove for days is highly nutritious, and when it is topped off with a generous portion of uncooked kimchi, it makes a healthy and hearty meal. Small portions of noodles or rice can be added to this mixture.

A serving of kimchi contains important minerals and vitamins such as manganese and folate (for brain health), Vitamins C, K, and A (for liver health), and B6 (for mood disorders, PMS, and morning sickness). Studies have shown kimchi to be beneficial for Type II Diabetes, asthmatics, and overweight individuals. It also improves cholesterol and blood pressure levels.

● Recipe #13: Kimchi

This recipe is a bit different with Brussels sprouts and fennel. You can create your own favorite combinations and use the same recipe by keeping the proportions relatively similar with the amount of vegetables to salt and sugar.

Ingredients:

2 lbs. (1 kg) Brussels sprouts, shredded
1 whole fennel root, julienned
1 grated apple or pear
½ cup (120 mL) sea salt
5 cloves garlic
1 inch (2½ cm) ginger root, peeled and thinly sliced
2 T (30 mL) fish sauce
1-3 T (15-45 mL) chili powder (to taste)
1 daikon radish, peeled and grated
4 scallions, chopped
1 T (15 mL) sugar (optional)
1 probiotic packet or capsule

Directions:

1. Dissolve ½ cup (120 mL) salt in enough water to cover the vegetables.
2. Soak for 4-6 hours. The longer the soak, the saltier the outcome.
3. Place all of the other ingredients in the mixture and stir the entire batch until it is mixed well.
4. Place in clean, sterilized jars. Add weights to keep all the ingredients below the water level.
5. If any small bits rise to the surface (and even if they don't), they typically create a white layer of film or even fuzz on the surface of the water. Use a clean paper towel or tissue to wipe this away over the one-week fermenting period.
6. With a marker, write the date of the ferment on the outside of the jar.
7. Wipe the lip of the jar with a clean cloth, then cover the jar with a coffee filter or another clean cloth and secure with a rubber band, to prevent insects from entering. This also leaves the air to circulate and encourage ferment.
8. Leave to sit on the kitchen counter (out of sunlight) for about a week.
9. Taste it, and when it is ready, jar it up and refrigerate it until consumed.

• Recipe #14: Pickled Carrots

Ingredients:

1 quart (1 L) carrots, sliced 1/4" thick, from about 1 lb. (½ kg) carrots
1 T (15 mL) fresh ginger, peeled and thinly sliced
1 T (15 mL) lime zest (absolutely no white pith!)
2 tsp (10 mL) pickling salt

Method:

1. Pack the carrots, ginger, and zest in the jars, leaving ½ inch (1 cm) headspace at the top.
2. Set aside.
3. Combine salt and water in a nonreactive saucepan and bring to a boil.
4. Reduce heat and simmer for 5 minutes.
5. Cool to room temperature.
6. Carefully ladle the liquid into the jars, leaving 1 inch (2½ cm) of headspace in each. With fermenting foods, keeping them below the liquid level prevents the food from getting moldy. If you have glass weights ("Pickle Pebbles"), add them to keep the carrots (or any other foodstuffs) below the water or liquid level. Make sure to leave breathing room at the top of the jar. (See Chapter 12 for where to purchase the Pickle Pebbles.)
7. Cover with the Pickle Pipe lid or a piece of cheesecloth. (Pickle Pipes are one-way airlocks that enable carbon dioxide to escape without allowing bugs or other contaminants to come into the environment. See Chapter 12 for where to buy them.)
8. Secure the jar with the jar's O-ring.
9. Place in a dark spot that hovers between 65°F and 75°F and leave for five days, checking daily to remove that white mold that accumulates on top.
10. Remove the Pickle Pipe or cheesecloth, cap the jars with regular lids, and refrigerate. (Carrots will keep for 2-3 weeks, refrigerated.)

● Recipe #15: Fermented Fruit Ketchup

Ketchup has not always been made with tomatoes. We can make great sweet/savory sauces as a condiment with any fruit. It goes amazingly well with any fish or chicken dishes, even cheese and crackers.

Let it ferment on the countertop for a week, then refrigerate it to stop the fermentation process. If you make a big batch, freeze leftovers (more than a glass jar full) in an ice cube tray and then store the cubes in a freezer bag until needed. Bacteria will hibernate and not die in the freezer.

Ingredients:

2 cups (500 mL) fruit of any type (including mango, berries, apples, and pears)
¼ cup (60 mL) granulated sugar
¼ (60 mL) dry white wine
¼ cup (60 mL) cider vinegar
1 tsp (5 mL) ground ginger
½ tsp (2½ mL) salt
½ tsp (2½ mL) dry mustard
¼ tsp (1 mL) each of ground allspice, cloves, and mustard

Method:

1. Combine fruit, sugar, wine, vinegar, salt, and spices in a small pot. Simmer for five minutes, stirring several times.
2. Fill large fermenting jars with fermentation lids and leave to ferment at room temperature for 1 week. Check daily and wipe white the mold off every day with a clean paper towel.
3. When it is to taste, transfer to smaller jars and refrigerate or freeze in small cubes and store frozen in small bags. Use as one would with regular ketchup, and with fish and chicken.

Chapter 11—Key Highlights:

1. Increase the positive microbial culture in your body by eating probiotics and prebiotics

2. Heal your leaky gut and decrease inflammation by increasing your intake of fermented foods and fiber at each meal.

3. Repair and replenish the mucosal lining of your gut by using bone broth to fill spaces or leaks.

4. Reduce or eliminate gluten from your diet by finding suitable substitutions. Add vegetables, fermented foods, and fermented condiments to your meals. Some examples of foods to eat include:

   - Mustard, ketchup, pesto, and mayonnaise
   - Pickled vegetables, kimchi, or sauerkraut
   - Yogurts, kefirs, and cheeses

5. Kefir products are made to contain over 15 different varieties of microbes, bacteria, yeasts, fungi, and protozoa, which will help you build a wider variety of organisms in your gut system as well as provide you with many other health benefits.

6. Fermented drinks (such as kombucha) and fermented vegetables (such as kimchi, pickled carrots, and fermented ketchup) have many health benefits. For example, kimchi is great for improving brain and liver health as well as for treating mood disorders, PMS, and morning sickness. Kimchi improves cholesterol and blood pressure levels. It is also beneficial for people who have Type II Diabetes, asthma, and/or are overweight.

7. Bacteria will hibernate and not die in the freezer.

Chapter 12: What's Next? (+ Resources)

There are many different things you can start doing to improve your health, as discussed throughout this book. *The Food-Mood Connection: A Holistic Approach to Understanding the Gut-Brain-Microbiome Relationship* explains the absolute importance of caring for and feeding your own unique microbiome. Part of this care includes changing your eating habits, your buying habits, your thoughts, and your behaviors. If we always do what we've always done, we'll just get what we always got! Pivot—change it up to achieve something new.

Often, changing any one of these aspects is difficult to do. Hypnotherapy makes it easier. As a certified hypnotherapist who holds many qualifications and university degrees, I can help you even further! You CAN live the life you want to live!

In this chapter, I have even put together a list of resources for you, in case you don't know where to begin! The first entries on this list of resources for you are the different ways you can find me. At present time, I can be found easily on the Internet, particularly through my website and Facebook. I am planning on having a presence on Instagram as well.

Contact Information

My office address is: #406-1755 West Broadway, Vancouver BC, Canada, V6J 4S5.

Telephone: 604-376-5932

Go to https://calendly.com/lynnepotterlord/30mins to schedule a 30-minute consultation (for FREE!) with me.

My hypnosis website is www.pivotal-hypnotherapy.com. There, you can find detailed information on more possibilities for using hypnosis and the gut-brain-microbiome connection.

Emails can be sent to lynne@pivotal-hypnotherapy.com.

"Like" my Facebook business page called Pivotal Hypnotherapy Vancouver. Find it at https://www.facebook.com/GutBrainHypnotist.

Connect with me on Facebook at https://www.facebook.com/lynne.p.lord/ (my personal profile).

Feel free to join my Facebook group called Pivotal Hypnotherapy Member's Group. This will be a central place where I will be holding Facebook Lives, free webinars and special events. If you care to learn more, please join and invite your friends. I guarantee it will be worth your while.

Follow me on Instagram: @pivotal_hypnotherapy.

Courses

I currently have two courses underway on the Podia.com platform, where my school is called "Lynne Potter Lord Academy" at https://lynnepotterlord.podia.com/. At the time of this writing, they are under development, but will go live shortly. (Depending on when you bought this book, everything might already be done!)

My classes are in the Lynne Potter Lord Academy:

- Course #1: The Food-Mood Connection: A Holistic Approach to the Gut-Brain-Microbiome Relationship
- Course #2: Ascension Meditation: Beginner 7th Path 1st-5th
- Course #3: Ascension Meditation: Advanced 7th Path 6th-9th
- Course #4: The Secret Language of Feelings

My book will be available and promoted on:

- http://www.thefood-moodconnection.com
- http://thegutbrainhypnotist.com

Videos

There are six really great informative videos on the site called International Scientific Association for Probiotics and Prebiotics (ISPPA).

The titles of the videos are:

- What is a Probiotic?
- What is a Prebiotic?
- What are Fermented Foods?
- Are all probiotics the same?
- How to choose a probiotic
- Health benefits of probiotics

Find the videos at https://isappscience.org/.

Transcripts of the videos are also available, right below the videos. The videos are all approximately two to three minutes in length and very informative. I highly suggest checking them out, to enhance your knowledge on these subjects. They are also great for using as hooks or openings if you do presentations.

COVID-19 and Probiotics

As I suggested in some passages, with our gut and other bodily microbiomes being so integral in our immunity, it makes perfect sense that microbiome research and study would commence in how it can be related to such a powerful virus as COVID-19. Several studies are listed on this website, showing research into the predictive outcome nature of microbial communities, vaccine development, as a "biotherapeutic product," and as a prevention measure alongside of the microbes in gut and nasal passages.

Further information can be seen at: https://isappscience.org/how-some-probiotic-and-prebiotic-scientists-are-working-to-address-covid-19/

Recordings

Visit https://soundcloud.com/lynne-potter-lord to download my COVID-19 relaxation recording(s) for free.

Visit https://www.pivotal-hypnotherapy.com/ for the COVID-specific recording that is on all pages of my website.

Kitchen Equipment and Ingredients

I definitely have my preferred resources for ingredients and equipment. I prefer to support local small businesses and encourage you to do so as well.

Having said that, I use the Internet to buy things, and admittedly, I buy items on Amazon. However, living in Canada adds a substantial charge to everything—even when they are labelled "free shipping" if shipped to the United States. I am fortunate enough to have an address in Bellingham, Washington, but for those of you who are not so lucky, I would seek out suppliers in Canada if you are in this country. Much of this equipment was difficult to find years ago when I started out, but it is much easier and more commonplace now.

Bacterial Starter Cultures

The key for homemade fermented food is quality bacterial starter cultures. Although you can "seed" these with a bit of leftovers from the last ½ cup (120 mL) of yogurt, kefir, kombucha, and the like, many feel safer with a fresh starter.

Visit http://caldwellbiofermentation.com/starter-culture.html—Caldwell's, a Canadian supplier. Mostly for vegetable ferments, Caldwell's has a long-standing relationship with Agriculture Canada and research therein.

Visit https://www.culturesforhealth.com/ for starter cultures (and equipment) for probiotic foods. It's a great site to shop and learn about all the foods, the process of getting them going, maintaining and storing the finished products, obtaining the proper equipment, DIY kits, how-to videos, and recipes.

Jars

Wide-mouth canning jars (preferred) in various heights are great for fermenting small-sized or medium-sized batches of fermented foods. Simple Internet searches will reveal local suppliers. Good quality jars are Bernardin, Ball, Mason, and Weck. Using canning jars ensures they are more utilitarian and shatterproof—and will last a lifetime, if cared for.

Larger jars such as greater than ½ gallon or gallon (1 L)) will need special lids and fermentation valves such as used in wine or beer making.

Fermentation Accessories

For fermentation equipment, full fermentation kits, Pickle Pipes, Pickle Pebbles, Kombucha, Kefir lids, and more can be purchased singly, in sets, or in kits on my site at www.food-moodconnection.com. I am keen to encourage others to ferment foods. It is something I am passionate to support. Small kits and lids can be purchased online here. Larger fermentation valves will also be available.

Sustainable Containers and Kits

Visit https://ecolunchboxes.com/collections/lunch-boxes for lunch kits with containers that fit together and don't leak are worth the investment (unless your kids lose them, so LABEL them). You can also find them on Amazon by searching for "Leak-proof lunchboxes."

Many local grocery stores will bring in other brands. It is great to buy locally, if you can. Ask your grocer or health food store for best cooperation.

FINAL WORDS

Whatever you do, remember to feed and care for your microbiome. Increase your fiber intake—gradually, if your body is not used to it. Your health and mood will improve if you consume healthy foods that nurture the good bugs in your body.

At this point, closing in to the end of the book, I would like to sincerely thank you for reading it. I would also like to acknowledge that there is a lot of information in it, and some of it reads like a textbook. (I know!) If you found it valuable, I encourage you to pass it on for others to read. I also very much appreciate your feedback and any time you enjoy my offerings, please let me know. I am excited for the possibilities for our healthy future!

Suggested Reading List

The Secret Language of Feelings: A Rational Approach to Emotional Mastery by Calvin Banyan

The Well-Fed Microbiome Cookbook: Vital Microbiome Diet Recipes to Repair and Renew the Body and Brain by Kristina Campbell

You Can Heal Your Life by Louise L. Hay

The UltraMind Solution: The Simple Way to Defeat Depression, Overcome Anxiety, and Sharpen Your Mind by Mark Hyman, M.D.

Eat Fat Get Thin: The Surprising Truth About the Fat We Eat—The Key to Sustained Weight Loss and Vibrant Health by Mark Hyman, M.D.

Brain Changer: The Good Mental Health Diet by Felice Jacka

Follow Your Gut: The Enormous Impact of Tiny Microbes by Rob Knight

KetoFast Cookbook by Dr. Joseph Mercola and Pete Evans

Probiotics for Health: 100 Amazing and Unexpected Uses for Probiotics by Jo A. Panyko

The Secret Life of Your Microbiome: Why Nature and Biodiversity are Essential to Health and Happiness by Susan L. Prescott

The Antianxiety Food Solution: How the Foods You Eat Can Help You Calm Your Anxious Mind, Improve Your Mood, and End Cravings by Trudy Scott, CN

The Good Gut: Taking Control of Your Weight, Your Mood, and Your Long-Term Health by Justin Sonnenburg and Erica Sonnenburg, PhDs

The Skinny Gut Diet: Balance Your Digestive System for Permanent Weight Loss by Brenda Watson

References

1. https://embryo.asu.edu/pages/ilya-ilyich-mechnikov-elie-metchnikoff-1845-1916

2. https://foodandmoodcentre.com.au

3. https://www.khanacademy.org/science/biology/cell-signaling/signaling-between-single-celled-organisms/a/cell-cell-signaling-in-unicellular-organisms

4. https://www.brainpickings.org/2016/09/26/the-hidden-life-of-trees-peter-wohlleben/

5. https://www.nature.com/news/scientists-bust-myth-that-our-bodies-have-more-bacteria-than-human-cells-1.19136

6. *The Botany of Desire: A Plant's-Eye View of the World* by Michael Pollan

7. https://ghr.nlm.nih.gov/primer/hgp/description

8. https://anesthesiology.duke.edu/?p=846744

9. https://msystems.asm.org/content/3/3/e00031-18

10. https://www.youtube.com/watch?v=awtmTJW9ic8

11. https://gem.cbc.ca/media/the-nature-of-things/season-55/episode-3/38e815a-0091c386082

12. https://www.spectrumnews.org/conference-news/international-society-Autism-research-2019/

13. https://www.spectrumnews.org/news/gut-woes-common-not-unique-among-children-Autism/

14. http://www.acs.org/content/acs/en/education/whatischemistry/landmarks/flemingpenicillin.html

15. http://www.fao.org/3/a-a0512e.pdf

16. *Brain Maker: The Power of Gut Microbes to Heal and Protect Your Brain for Life* by David Perlmutter

17. https://canadiancoursereadings.ca/product/secret-life-of-your-microbiome/

18. Skin https://www.ncbi.nlm.nih.gov/pmc/articles/PMC6518061/

19. Cold/Flu https://www.medicalnewstoday.com/articles/324180#Probiotics-for-your-respiratory-system

20. Colic https://pubmed.ncbi.nlm.nih.gov/32053826/

21. http://www.probioticchart.ca/?utm_source=intro_pg&utm_medium=civ&utm_campaign=CDN_CHART

22. *Cooked: A Natural History of Transformation* by Michael Pollan

23. *Eat Dirt: Why Leaky Gut May Be the Root Cause of Your Health Problems and 5 Surprising Steps on How to Cure It* by Dr. Josh Axe

24. https://www.scientificamerican.com/article/ultimate-social-network-bacteria-protects-health/ by Jennifer Ackerman (June 2012 article, pp.37-43—as at May 1, 2020.)

25. https://www.huffpost.com/entry/hand-washing-dishes-benefits_n_6736636

26. https://www.ncbi.nlm.nih.gov/pubmed/21248165

27. ALS https://docs.google.com/document/d/11feGbUrN81v51NijlmfeOQW9UVIrMcTbJkVk5y7JKZI/edit (access must be requested to view this)

28. Alzheimer's https://www.ncbi.nlm.nih.gov/pubmed/24138599

29. Anxiety and Depression https://www.ncbi.nlm.nih.gov/pubmed/26528128

30. ADHD https://www.ncbi.nlm.nih.gov/pubmed/25599186,

31. Autism https://www.ncbi.nlm.nih.gov/pubmed/25262969%20,

32. Candida https://www.sciencedirect.com/science/article/pii/S128645791400077X

33. Celiac https://www.ncbi.nlm.nih.gov/pubmed/22583600%20,

34. Chronic Fatigue https://www.ncbi.nlm.nih.gov/pubmed/17007934,

35. Crohn's https://www.ncbi.nlm.nih.gov/pubmed/24969297,

36. Fibromyalgia https://www.ncbi.nlm.nih.gov/pubmed/18540025,

37. Gas, Bloating, Digestive Pain https://www.ncbi.nlm.nih.gov/pubmed/26491416,

38. Hashimoto's https://www.ncbi.nlm.nih.gov/pubmed/18777226,

39. IBS https://www.ncbi.nlm.nih.gov/pmc/articles/PMC5595063/,/

40. Lupus https://www.ncbi.nlm.nih.gov/pmc/articles/PMC1753363/,/

41. Metabolic Syndrome https://www.ncbi.nlm.nih.gov/pubmed/26459447%20,

42. Migraine https://www.ncbi.nlm.nih.gov/pubmed/28537581,

43. MS https://www.ncbi.nlm.nih.gov/pubmed/25184418,

44. NAFLD https://www.ncbi.nlm.nih.gov/pubmed/26447960,

45. Parkinson's https://www.ncbi.nlm.nih.gov/pubmed/221450

46. Restless Leg, etc. https://www.ncbi.nlm.nih.gov/pubmed/3745938,

47. Type 1 Diabetes, https://www.ncbi.nlm.nih.gov/pubmed/26269193,

48. Type 2, Colitis https://onlinelibrary.wiley.com/doi/10.1002/9783527692156.ch47

49. Allergies and Food Sensitivities https://www.ncbi.nlm.nih.gov/pubmed/26456445

50. http://www.fao.org/nutrition/education/food-based-dietary-guidelines/regions/countries/brazil/en/

51. https://food-guide.canada.ca/en/

52. https://www.huffpost.com/entry/food-pyramid-usda_n_870375?guccounter=1&guce_referrer=aHR0cHM6Ly93d3cuZ29vZ2xlLmNvbbS8&guce_referrer_sig=AQAAAEQbhim1y3VQhnZtNXSQfVtaG5JoTWkZa-kuXS5Yyvh47WnarqjYwOD7errKJVEN2HqqqrZlMQnFqXXd2sfeMHadUssewoXy4diQbhZTq1vfKmLnvF6IuGXbqYAEi8_18SaDVxhdmpyYZWw0OOPytU8wzkdOAEPtcdZa7kOrHLH.

53. http://www.fao.org/nutrition/education/food-based-dietary-guidelines/regions/countries/brazil/en/

54. https://www.cbc.ca/news/health/canada-food-guide-unveil-1.4987261

55. https://www.healthline.com/nutrition/10-health-benefits-of-apples#section4

56. https://www.hindawi.com/journals/ad/2014/152428/

57. http://guidelines.Diabetes.ca/docs/cpg/Ch35-Type-2-Diabetes-in-Children-and-Adolescents.pdf

58. https://www.thehealthsite.com/diseases-conditions/type-3-Diabetes-insulin-resistance-in-brain-causes-alzheimers-disease-684916/

59. https://sugarscience.ucsf.edu/hidden-in-plain-sight/#.Xrhu5xNKjUo

60. https://celiac.org/about-celiac-disease/related-conditions/autoimmune-disorders/

61. https://www.spectrumnews.org/conference-news/international-society-Autism-research-2019/

62. https://www.ncbi.nlm.nih.gov/pmc/articles/PMC4290017/

63. https://www.ncbi.nlm.nih.gov/pmc/articles/PMC6213508/

64. https://www.newyorker.com/magazine/2003/11/10/the-reeve-effect

65. https://people.com/celebrity/woman-who-had-half-her-brain-removed-defies-the-odds-gets-a-masters-degree/

66. *The Woman Who Changed Her Brain: And Other Inspiring Stories of Pioneering Brain Transformation* by Barbara Arrowsmith

67. http://faculty.fortlewis.edu/burke_b/personality/Readings/AdaptiveUnconscious.pdf

68. *Catharsis in Regression Hypnotherapy: Transcripts of Transformation, Volume II* by Calvin Banyan (5-Path.com)

69. *Brain Maker: The Power of Gut Microbes to Heal and Protect Your Brain for Life* by David Perlmutter

70. https://www.usatoday.com/story/news/humankind/2016/01/12/teen-girl-uses-crazy-strength-lift-burning-car-off-dad/78675898/.

71. https://www.healthline.com/nutrition/gut-brain-connection

72. https://www.scientificamerican.com/article/what-is-the-function-of-t-1997-12-22/

73. http://johnmongiovi.com/blog/2014/10/22/a-history-of-hypnosis-from-ancient-temples-to-modern-psychology

74. https://yogasynergy.com/true-meaning-meditation-isyoga/

75. https://www.latimes.com/archives/la-xpm-2008-feb-06-me-maharishi06-story.html

76. https://ca.tm.org/en/?gclid=Cj0KCQiAxfzvBRCZARIsAGA7YMwy9Qa0poJLYAGeJDqj6Rmuui2BzsrFi8U7YBNwBMm9Mf_9jrTkxSIaAr94EALw_wcB#benefits

77. https://www.webmd.com/mental-health/qa/what-is-hypnotherapy

78. https://www.brainpickings.org/2014/01/29/carol-dweck-mindset/

79. https://www.youtube.com/watch?v=IGQmdoK_ZfY

80. *Brain Maker: The Power of Gut Microbes to Heal and Protect Your Brain for Life* by David Perlmutter

81. *Gut and Psychology Syndrome: Natural Treatment for Autism, Dyspraxia, A.D.D., Dyslexia, A.D.H.D., Depression, and Schizophrenia* by Dr. Natasha Campbell-McBride

82. https://foodandmoodcentre.com.au/)

83. *Fat for Fuel: A Revolutionary Diet to Combat Cancer, Boost Brain Power, and Increase Your Energy* by Dr. Joseph Mercola

84. https://www.ncbi.nlm.nih.gov/pubmed/31010014

85. https://www.Autismspeaks.ca/about-Autism/treatment/treatments-for-associated-medical-conditions/gi-disorders/

86. https://Autismcanada.org/living-with-Autism/treatments/biomedical/diets/gluten-free/

87. https://www.health.harvard.edu/mind-and-mood/probiotics-may-help-boost-mood-and-cognitive-function

88. https://www.ncbi.nlm.nih.gov/pmc/articles/PMC3970207/

89. https://www.Autismspeaks.org/science-news/cdc-increases-estimate-Autisms-prevalence-15-percent-1-59-children.

90. https://www.ncbi.nlm.nih.gov/pmc/articles/PMC4442490/

91. *Brain Maker: The Power of Gut Microbes to Heal and Protect Your Brain for Life* by David Perlmutter

92. Food: What the Heck Should I Eat? by Mark Hyman, M.D.

93. https://www.ncbi.nlm.nih.gov/pmc/articles/PMC6013535/

94. https://care.diabetesjournals.org/content/38/1/159

95. https://www.louisehay.com/

96. https://www.eftuniverse.com/

97. https://www.thetappingsolution.com/

98. https://www.emofree.com/

99. https://www.youtube.com/watch?v=XRfLTQjJhp0

100. *Friend of a Friend…: Understanding the Hidden Networks That Can Transform Your Life and Your Career* by David Burkus

101. https://www.classaction.com/roundup-weed-killer/lawsuit/April 1/2020

102. https://www.foodpolitics.com/2018/06/biggest-global-food-companies-according-to-forbes/.

103. https://www.theguardian.com/environment/2017/sep/12/third-of-earths-soil-acutely-degraded-due-to-agriculture-study

104. https://www.extension.purdue.edu/extmedia/WQ/WQ-7.html

105. https://sciencenordic.com/allergies-childrens-health-forskningno/much-less-allergy-in-families-who-do-the-dishes-by-hand/1414742

106. https://toriavey.com/home-garden/natural-all-purpose-homemade-citrus-cleanser/

107. https://www.preparedsociety.com/threads/pros-and-cons-of-a-100-mile-diet.2078/.

108. https://www.health.harvard.edu/blog/backyard-gardening-grow-your-own-food-improve-your-health-201206294984

109. https://foodandmoodcentre.com.au/2016/07/diet-and-mental-health-in-children-and-adolescents/

110. https://www.health.harvard.edu/blog/intermittent-fasting-surprising-update-2018062914156

About the Author

Lynne Potter Lord was born in Vancouver, B.C. and lives in a heritage house near the beach, with her partner their dog, and their cat. Her interests include reading, writing, studying, painting, knitting, and making all sorts of things.

Lynne owns Pivotal Hypnotherapy, her hypnosis practice, where she teaches others how to change their thoughts, feelings, and behaviors, and develop new mindsets. Lynne does this by using modern techniques as well as a foundational understanding of food and the gut-brain connection. Clients are enabled to do everything from breaking everyday bad habits to creating new lives—free of pain, anxiety, depression, addictions, cravings, and compulsions. She also works with clients who want to improve their already great lives or who want to be better, by enhancing things that already work. After working with Lynne, people are grateful their lives include better sleep, better health, more joy, enhanced skills, and life satisfaction!

With her debut book, *The Food-Mood Connection: A Holistic Approach to Understanding the Gut-Brain-Microbiome Relationship,* Lynne hopes readers will understand that we have much more control over our own physical and mental health and our personal growth than we realize. Harnessing the power of the gut-brain connection by using both our first and second brains can greatly enhance and improve our health and wellness. At the same time, some small changes in habits at the individual level can accumulate and really change the entire world. Now is the time, when we are all on the same level playing field, that we can realize and achieve a global vision of health, and Lynne wants you to do your part.

NOTES

_____

_____

_____

_____

_____

_____

_____

_____

_____

_____

_____

_____

_____

_____

_____

_____

_____

_____

_____

_____

_____

Made in the USA
Monee, IL
13 September 2020